D1065453

The Secret of a Happy
Wedded Life

The Secret of a Happy Wedded Life

Thoughts, Truths, Anecdotes, Verse and Helps
for Everyone's Inspiration

By

W. G. Heslop, Litt. S.D., D.D.

Pastor, Church of the Nazarene
Grand Rapids, Michigan

Author of:
"Gems from Genesis," etc.

ZONDERVAN PUBLISHING HOUSE
Grand Rapids, Michigan

CONTENTS

		Page
I.	Love	7
II.	Marriage	18
III.	Home	26
IV.	Children	40
V.	Helps to Husbands	92
VI.	Words of Wisdom to Wives	98
VII.	Thoughts from Other Thinkers	106

CHAPTER I

LOVE

ALL love is of God. Satan knows nothing about love of any kind. The Devil is filled with hate and unholiness. He is the blaster and blighter of all beauty in spirit, soul and body. God is love. To love is to be like God. Love is everything and is worth everything. The human race loves, admires, respects and appreciates a lover. The religion of Jesus Christ is a religion of love; it is a love religion.

Love is the fulfilling of all law. Love is Heaven's law and Heaven's happiness. Paradise here or elsewhere, now or in the future, is impossible without love. Perdition is a place where love is absent. A loveless heart is hell begun on earth. Only love understands love. It needs no gifts and needs no words. Itself is the most acceptable gift and it speaks the loudest where it is the fullest. Men and women who insinuate that love makes fools of us all are mistaken. Ignorance and misunderstanding, sentiment and foolish actions may make fools of us all, but love is wisdom and the only lasting wisdom. It is simply not true that in love we are all fools alike. Sentiment and emotion uncontrolled may force a person into a foolish and questionable attitude, but love is heaven's harmony and hell's confusion.

Love is the sweetest flower in the garden of God, for He himself is love. Real love is the wine and the elixir of existence. It makes a true martyr of all those in whose breast it is allowed to swell and enlarge. Love can and does dispel the darkness of night and the despair of the lonesome. Love makes men akin to God and holiness and angels.

Satan and demons know nothing of it and cannot imitate it. Love is the breath from heaven and its absence is the beginning of hell. Only the brave and beautiful truly love and nobly live.

* * * *

"I have one more word of advice to give," once said Talmage, "to those who would have a happy home, and that is, let love preside in it. When your behavior in the domestic circle becomes a mere matter of calculation; when the caress you give is merely the result of deliberate study of the position you occupy, happiness lies stark dead on the hearthstone. When the husband's position as head of the household is maintained by loudness of voice, by strength of arm, by fire of temper, the republic of domestic bliss has become a despotism that neither God nor man will abide. Oh, ye who promised to love each other at the altar, how dare you commit perjury? Let no shadow of suspicion come on your affection. It is easier to kill that flower than it is to make it live again. The blast from hell that puts out that light leaves you in the blackness of darkness forever."

* * * *

A young woman who runs a power sewing machine for fifty hours a week in a factory tells the following story of her married life: "My husband, left an orphan, never had a chance to go to school or learn a trade. He is a teamster and makes very little money, but he loves me enough to trust me with all he earns. My husband does not go to saloons or places of that sort, and he never goes out for pleasure without me. Do you think it hurts me that he can't give me fine clothes when every day he tells me I am the best thing God ever gave him? Every night he kisses my hands that have worked so hard all day. We have been married over a year and never a cross word. I did not know any one could be so happy. Do you think I mind working to help a man like that? His love makes everything worth while." Here is a man, ignorant of books, with no business training, yet possessing the rare faculty that guides his home-life in ways of happiness and peace.

* * * *

Henry Van Dyne wrote the lovely lines,
"I read within a poet's book
A word that starred the page,
'Stone walls do not a prison make,
Nor iron bars a cage.'
Yes, that is true, and something more:
You'll find where'er you roam,
That marble floors and gilded walls
Can never make a home.
But every house where love abides
And friendship is a guest,
Is surely home, and home, sweet home;
For there the heart can rest."

* * * *

A large portion of the true life of a human being is made up of loving sympathy and loving deeds; and when instead of love there is indifference and peevishness and discontent and disgust, of course health must fail. A single gravel stone in the shoe hurts more than a cart load in a gravel pit. A single speck of dust in the eye causes more discomfort than a bushel would flying in the open air. So the little faults and discomforts in the sacred precincts of home, are an affliction compared with which outside troubles are very light; and slight differences among those who are linked together in the closest ties, become an occasion of great trial and discomfort.

*   *   *   *

Like virtue, honesty and truthfulness, love is its own reward, while hate, dishonesty, untruthfulness and sin accomplish their own ruin. The love of God to man and man to God and man to man is the divinest and sweetest thing in all the world of sin and war. Love never loses; love always wins; love always lasts. It defies all sophistries and despite the depravity and deviltry on every hand love finally must triumph for love is of God. In suffering for one upon whom we bestow our love, our very aches and pains, our misery and weariness grows dearer to us. No age, condition or circumstance should be allowed to freeze the deep well of love in our hearts. All love-less people are old people. The loving and lovable are always young.

Love is not an idea or a sentiment but a soul. God breathed into man the breath of life and man became a living and loving soul and only sin can slay such a divinity.

No disguise can possibly conceal love where it is, and no hypocrisy can feign it where it is not. Love gives wings to the life of the man or woman in whose heart it is allowed to grow, flourish and bring forth fruit. Love lifts loads from the heart and places them upon the shoulder, thus making the steps lighter, hammering springs in the heels of our fellow travellers on the highway of life. Love is the entire history of our God and the more Godlike we become the more we shall love even though the less we may be loved. The highest love is to love because it is Godlike, to love because it is Divine, to love for the sake of loving.

Riches are ruined by rust. They oftimes take to themselves wings and fly away, comforts and consolations soon vanish, even hope may become dimmed, but love stays and strengthens. It never fails, for love is of God. All hatred was and is satanic and hellish while all love and holiness is of God and heavenly.

* * * *

"O, glorious! Would to God I had a wife such as this!" is the written comment on Proverbs 31 (the description of the virtuous woman) which was discovered in the great Lord Shaftesbury's pocket-Bible. A later note which follows reads thus: "And so I have, God be everlastingly praised! 1846."

* * * *

"I am sure," wrote Horace Bushnell, "that there is nothing more beautiful and more to be envied by the

poets than this same charm of power by which a good
wife detains her husband. It is not an ambitious, noisy
power; it is silent, calm, persuasive, and often so deep
as to have its hold deeper than consciousness itself. He
is proud of her without knowing it, loves her when he
is too weary or too much bent on his objects to be
conscious of his love, deposits his soul in hers and
thinks it still his own. She ministers, and yet is seldom
ministered unto. She makes his future and ascribes it
to himself."

* * * *

In *"Nathaniel Hawthorne and His Wife"* we realize
how perfect a marriage can be where there is love
and intellectual companionship. The constant inter-
change of confidence in these two lives brought that
perfection of relation which is the first essential of an
ideal home, where love loses itself in filling the offices
of love. It is said of Mrs. Hawthorne that in her relations as his wife she acted instinctively, not from a
settled purpose — unconsciously, not designedly. As
she made the ideal wife, so did he a husband. "He
was not, as so many men are, a merely passive and
complacent absorber of all this devotion. What she
gave he returned; she never touched him without a
response; she never called to him without an echo."

* * * *

A woman lived in Georgia, who had kept a vow of
silence thirty years. Her husband returned from business one day in a nervous excitable mood. She began
to tell him about some of her annoyances, when he

suddenly bade her be quiet, nor let the sound of her voice be heard. She felt grieved beyond endurance and vowed he should never again hear her voice. He never did, nor did any one else. She performed her daily duties in silence. If anything had to be said, she wrote on a slate. In spite of penitence, appeals, entreaties, she kept her vow. Before her husband died he begged her but to say she had forgiven him; she wrote on a slate. She died, a few years ago, without having uttered a word, and was thus taken from the battle ground of a thirty-year's war.

*   *   *   *

Who has not read with thrilling interest the story of old curfew? A young soldier for some offense was condemned to die, and the time of his death was fixed "at the ringing of the curfew." Naturally such a doom would be fearful and bitter to one in the years of his hope and prime; but to this unhappy youth death was doubly terrible, since he was soon to marry a beautiful young lady, whom he had long loved. The lady, who loved him ardently in return, had used her utmost efforts to avert his fate, pleading with the judges and even with Cromwell himself; but all in vain. In her despair she tried to bribe the old sexton not to ring the bell, but she found that to be impossible.

The hour for the execution drew near. The preparations were completed. The officers of the law brought forth the prisoner and waited, while the sun was setting, for the signal from the distant bell-tower.

To the wonder of everybody curfew did not ring!

Only one human being at that moment knew the reason. The poor girl, half wild with the thought of her lover's peril, had rushed unseen up the winding stairs, and climbed the ladders into the belfry-loft, and seized the tongue of the bell. The old sexton was in his place, prompt to the fatal moment. He threw his weight upon the rope, and the bell, obedient to his practised hand, reeled and swung to and fro in the tower. But the brave girl kept her hold, and no sound issued from its metallic lips. Again and again the sexton drew the rope, but with desperate strength the young heroine held on. Every moment made her position more fearful; every sway of the mighty bell threatened to fling her through the high tower window; but she would not let go.

At last the sexton went away. Old and deaf, he had not noticed that the curfew gave no peal. The brave girl descended from the belfry, wounded and trembling. She hurried from the church to the place of execution. Cromwell himself was there, and just as he was sending to demand why the bell was silent, she saw him —

"And her brow,
Lately white with sorrow, glows with hope and courage
now.
At his feet she told her story, showed her hands all
bruised and torn,
And her young face, still haggard with the anguish
it had worn,
Touched his heart with sudden pity, lit his eyes with
misty light —

'Go; your lover lives,' cried Cromwell; 'Curfew shall
not ring tonight.' "

Think you, that this young man, redeemed by that
sacrifice of love from the clutches of the law, would
regard any service to the fair woman who redeemed
him a hardship? Nay, he would have been willing to
have laid his life upon the altar for her.

"Now," says Dr. L. G. Broughton, "let us listen to
another story of love.

"The scene is laid at Calvary. Jesus is upon the
cross. The brow once crowned with glory is now
crowned with thorns. The hands so often outstretched
in love and mercy are now pinioned to the cross. The
heart that throbbed and ached with human sorrow is
now pierced with a spear. Oh, it is a sad moment in
the history of the world! The earth trembles, the
mountains quake, and the sun veils itself in darkness,
for God's Son is dying.

"But listen! 'It is finished! It is finished! It is
finished!'

"The great plan of redemption, born in the heart of
love, has now received its finishing touch, and God and
the world stand reconciled.

"Oh, dear friends, this was for us! Shall we not
respond, not only with our hearts, but with our sub-
stance — yea, with all that we have — to gladden His
dear heart and spread His kingdom from pole to pole?"

* * * *

True love is better than houses, lands, barns and
bungalows. That man is to be pitied in whose heart

love has never been born or in whose breast it has died. That woman is to be shunned in whose soul there burns no love. Love is wonderful and everlasting. All else shall pass away.

King David lamenting his youthful friend Jonathan once said, "Thy love to me was wonderful, passing the love of women." Such love is real life and noble living. The human heart filled with love is everlastingly guarded against the onslaughts of sin and satan. The present restlessness of the human race is not caused by a lack of luxury, a want of houses, furniture, or an automobile, but by the lack of love.

A person without love is a person in whose soul will soon blaze the fires of an ever increasing purgatory.

To love, faults and failings are either unseen or are transformed into beautiful and fragrant flowers, for love is an *alchemist*. To love is to be happy. To love more is to be happier. To love now is to be happy now. To love today is to be happy today. Without love life is not worth living. Life becomes less than nothing without a living, breathing, feeling and enlarging love. Love cannot be bought, for it comes from God.

It is a gift from Heaven and wherever absent, hell has already begun. The greatest pleasure of life is a heart expanding with love toward God, Christ, the Church and our fellow man. To say that love is blind is to express an untruth. Sentiment and uncontrolled emotion may be foolish and blind, but love is sight, love is life, love is living.

*   *   *   *

Have you ever read the lines of Strickland Gillilan on "Folks Need a Lot of Loving,"? here they are:

"Folks need a lot of loving in the morning;
    The day is all before, with cares beset—
The cares we know, and they that give no warning;
    For love is God's own antidote for fret.
"Folks need a heap of loving at the noontime—
    In the battle lull, the moment snatched from strife—
Half-way between the waking and the croontime,
    While bickering and worriment are rife.
"Folks hunger so for loving at the night-time,
    When wearily they take them home to rest—
At slumber-song and turning-out-the-light time—
    Of all the times for loving, that's the best!
"Folks want a lot of loving every minute—
    The sympathy of others and their smile!
Till life's end, from the moment they begin it,
    Folks need a lot of loving all the while."

* * * *

No cable can draw as forcibly and no cord can bind as securely as love can do with only a simple thread. If these words should reach the eyes and ears of one in whose heart love is dying or becoming cold, we would urge a place of prayer until the cooling heart is rekindled with the love of God for if love dies it is the worst of deaths. Hell is born wherever love dies.

CHAPTER II

MARRIAGE

MUTUAL love is the crown of all bliss and the capstone of all enduring loveliness. The most precious possession that a man ever inherits in this world apart from God and holiness is the heart of a noble girl or woman. The greatest treasure in the possession of a pure and winsome girl or woman is the sincere love of a happy and strong husband.

The Holy Bible opens with a holy pair in a paradise below. That paradise and that holiness was marred by sin and satan. It was true in the beginning and it is true today that "It is not good that the man should be alone."

Marriage was intended by a good and gracious God to be the bloom of all men's happiness as it is the heart of all holy desire of normal womanhood.

"What therefore God hath joined together let no man put asunder." Never dying fires are intended to be kindled in the combined hearts of bride and groom for of earthly possessions the best is a good and holy wife, and of earthly treasures the rarest is a strong, happy and unselfish husband.

Wedlock is intended by God to be a highway without either a left or a right turn or fork in the road. Stop-overs are not allowed, for marriages were made in heaven and are as lasting as life. Only the wise take to themselves a pure and holy wife and only the winsome and heavenly maiden will take to herself a happy, strong and holy protector. Riches and poverty are nothing. Goodness, truth and holiness are everything.

God made no provision for failure of the marriage relation for men may succeed and women may win.

* * * *

"Marriage is a failure," says the Springfield Times, "when either of the parties marries for money.

"When one of the parties engages in a business that is not approved by the other.

"When both parties persist in arguing over a subject upon which they never have and never can think alike.

"When children are obliged to clamor for their rights.

"When the watchword is: 'Each for himself.'

"When the money that should go for a book goes for what only one side of the house knows anything about.

"When politeness, fine manners and kindly attention are reserved for company or visits abroad."

* * * *

The Rev. Philip Henry used to give two pieces of advice to his children and others in reference to marriage. One was, "Keep within the bounds of profession." The other was, "Look at suitableness in age, quality, education, temper" etc. He used to observe, from Gen. 2:18, "I will make him an help meet for him," that where there is not meetness, there will not be much help. He commonly said to his children, with reference to their choice in marriage, "Please God, and please yourselves, and you shall never displease me;" and greatly blamed those parents who concluded matches for their children without their consent. He sometimes mentioned the saying of a pious gentlewoman, who had many daughters: "The care of most people is how to get good husbands for their daughters; but my care is to fit my daughters to be good wives, and then let God provide for them."

The Rev. S. Kilpin, of Exeter, had witnessed the awful consequences produced in the church of Christ, and in families, from those who professed to be the disciples of Jesus, forming marriages contrary to the command, — "Be not unequally yoked with unbe-lievers," — "only in the Lord," etc. As he never shunned to declare the whole counsel of God, this sub-ject was presented to his congregation. The next day, a gentleman, whose name or residence he never knew, called to thank him for the discourse, adding that his state of mind when he entered Exeter was most dis-tressing, as he was on the very point of complying with a dreadful temptation, which would have embittered his future life. He had been a disciple of Christ, was anxious to consecrate his life to the service of his adorable Master, and had sought a helpmate to strengthen his hands in serving God. A lady, whom he deemed pious, had accepted his addresses; but when every customary arrangement was made, she had dis-honorably discarded him. His mind was so exceedingly wounded and disgusted, that he had determined to choose a wife who made no profession of religion, and had fixed on another object for his addresses with every prospect of success, although he had not as yet men-

tioned his intention to her. He added, "But the providence of God led me, an entire stranger in this city, to
your meeting-house. You may suppose that your subject arrested my attention. You appeared to be
acquainted with every feeling of my soul. I saw my
danger and perceived the temptation and the certain
ruin of my peace if the dreadful snare had not been
broken. You, sir, under God, have been my deliverer.
By the next Sabbath I should have been bound in honor
to an enemy of that Jesus whom I adore; for although
she is moral and externally correct, yet she knows the
Savior only in name. I could not leave the city in peace
until I had sought to make this communication." They
unitedly addressed Him who can deliver, and does
deliver His people. Thus, while part of his congregation thought it an unfit subject for the pulpit, at least
one person received it as a message from God, by whom
it was no doubt sent.

* * * *

A young lady came from England to marry a young
man to whom she had been long engaged. Soon after
her arrival she learned that he had formed the habit of
drinking to excess. She told him she could not marry
him. He protested his love and promised to reform.
She answered nobly and firmly, "No, I dare not trust
my future happiness to a man who has formed such
a habit. I came three thousand miles to marry the man
I loved, but rather than marry a drunkard I will travel
three thousand back again." She kept her word, and

saved herself from a lifelong association with a loathsome drunkard.

* * * *

Rev. Philip Henry used to say, both to his children and others, in reference to marriage, "Keep within the bounds of profession; look at suitableness in age, quality, education, temper," etc. He used to observe, from Gen. 2:18, "I will make him a help-meet for him," that where there is not meetness, there will not be much help. He commonly said to his children, with reference to their choice in marriage, "Please God, and please yourselves, and you shall never displease me," and greatly blamed those parents who conclude matches for their children without their consent. He sometimes mentioned the saying of a pious woman, who had many daughters, "The care of most people is how to get good husbands for their daughters; but my care is to fit my daughters to be good wives, and then let God provide for them."

* * * *

The Cherokee marriage-ceremony is very expressive. The man and woman join hands over running water, to indicate that their lives are thenceforth to flow on in one stream.

* * * *

A consistent Christian young man became attached to a pleasure-loving and gay young lady, and married her against the advice of his brethren. Her influence silenced his prayers, estranged him from the house of God, and led him to her ways of pleasure. Sickness called his attention back to religion. Twice his wife had driven him from duty. Now, in agony and remorse, with a fearful eternity before him, he gazed upon her, and cried, "Rebecca, Rebecca, you are the cause of my eternal damnation!" and died.

* * * *

Woman was born to be the tender mate of a worthy man and in obedience to God, the will of God, and the laws of God, she best fulfills her destiny and the purposes of heaven.

The marriage of one man to one maid may be likened to a pair of scissors, so joined that they cannot be separated; sometimes moving in opposite directions but always coming together again and punishing all that come between them.

Marriage enlarges and expands the scene and scope of all the life. It should be a marriage of love and common interest. It should combine the pleasures of friendship with all the enjoyment of controlled sense and reason and sweeten the whole of life and its pursuits.

It is consummate foolishness to wait for a perfect mate for if one were found the other would be unfit.

* * * *

"A well-matched couple," declared Spurgeon, "carry a joyful life between them, as the two spies carried the cluster of Eshcol. They are a brace of birds of Paradise. They multiply their joys by sharing them, and lessen their troubles by dividing them. This is fine arithmetic. The wagon of care rolls lightly along as they pull together; and when it drags a little heavy, or there is a hitch anywhere, they love each other all the more, and so lighten the labor."

* * * *

Rev. Robert Newton, the Wesleyan pulpit orator, and his bride, began their married life by retiring twice each day to pray with and for each other. This practice they kept up, when opportunity served, to the end of life. When an old man, Mr. Newton remarked, "In the course of a short time, my wife and I shall celebrate the jubilee of our marriage; and I know not that, during the fifty years of our union, an unkind look or an unkind word has ever passed between us."

* * * *

Marriage is for the strong souled. Weaklings go to the wall and wail. To be well matched and well married gives wings to the life and labor. Marriage is to be a feast where the grace repeated at the table is the flavoring and the dinner a delight. All shin kicking should be shunned and all elbow punching should be studiously avoided. Husbands and wives may TALK of the miseries and woes of life, but it is the bachelor and the poodle-loving spinsters who BEAR them.

If a true man will choose a pure woman for qualities that will wear and endure rather than for paint and pleasure that is passing, the union should make a Paradise on earth.

In order to last for life the nuptial union must be

held fast by the bond of virtue, kindness and love. The only present bliss that seems to have survived the sin and fall of man is domestic happiness, the union of two hearts as one. No fortune can possibly compensate for the misfortune of an unhappy marriage. Within the small circle of the wedding ring there may be a happy heaven or an unmitigated unhappy hell. The union of a noble and winsome woman and a strong, true and manly man, is the entrance into a state of bliss that delights the heart of God, for marriage is of God. Wedlock was never intended to be a saucy, sad, familiar state where folks are apt to scold and hate. It is intended to be the union of two hearts that beat as one, four hands that work as one and four legs that walk as one. The bachelor, who, apart from the will of God, has made up his mind never to marry should die before he gets the chance to wed, and the canary and cat worshipping spinster should be sent to the Canary Islands.

The lines of latitude and longitude on the conjugal sea may never be traced except by those who truly love God and just as truly love another.

Marriage, while it is a real romance, was not planned to be romantic only. It was planned that a happy couple co-operate with their partner God in redeeming the world and blessing the race.

Chapter III

HOME

Happiness in the home is impossible without holiness in the heart. Selfishness is misery and suicide. Happiness in the married life is simply impossible except each in turn give up their pet humors and petty inclinations.

It is always true that "the kindest and happiest pair, will find occasion to forbear; and something every day they live, to pity and perhaps forgive."

The whole family must remember that each is virtually concerned with the happiness of the others. Each should seek to avoid the little offensive things in life for very small things may blast an infant blossom. Love is sensitive. It is easily hurt, easily grieved but just as easily forgives and forgets.

Home means life and living. It takes at least two to make a home, and a home takes time to build. It needs both Summer and Winter, snow and heat, frost and fire, Summer to ripen the rich and precious fruits and Winter to mellow and season the same. Home to be a real and happy home means a heap of living and loving, and, bearing and forebearing after the marriage vows have been taken before the minister. Thrice happy are those who enjoy a holy, uninterrupted union and whose love unbroken by complaints and unspoiled by criticisms, shall not dissolve until death. All contention and blame setting should be studiously avoided and each must seek to lighten each other's loads, share each other's woe and bear each other's burdens.

Domestic strife should never be allowed to discolor the dawn of a new day. It is senseless to fuss and stew about whether the mutton should be boiled or roasted and then fight even over the size of the slice. It is a tragedy when either lays up fuel for the fires of dissension, when either gathers together a magazine of provocations, when either seeks to exasperate the other.

*   *   *   *

"It takes a heap o' living' in a house t' make it home,
A heap o' sun an' shadder, an' ye sometimes have t' roam
Afore ye really 'preciate the things ye lef' behind,
An' hunger for 'em somehow, with 'em allus on yer mind.

It don't make any differunce how rich ye get t' be,
How much yer chairs an' tables cost, how great yer luxury;
It ain't home t' ye, though it be the palace of a king,
Until somehow yer soul is sort o' wrapped round everything.

"Home ain't a place that gold can buy or get up in a minute;
Afore it's home there's got t' be a heap o' livin' in it.
Within the walls there's got t' be some babies born, and then
Right there ye've got t' bring 'em up t' women good, an' men;
And gradjerly, as time goes on, ye find ye wouldn't part
With anything they ever used—they've grown into yer heart;
The old high chairs, the playthings, too, the little shoes they
   wore
Ye hoard; an' if ye could ye'd keep the thumbmarks on the door.

"Ye've got t' weep t' make it home, ye've got t' sit an' sigh
An' watch beside a loved one's bed, an' know that Death is nigh;
An' in the stillness o' the night t' see Death's angel come,
An' close the eyes o' her that smiled, an' leave her sweet voice
   dumb.

Fer these are scenes that grip the heart, an' when yer tears are
   dried,

Ye find the home is dearer than it was, an' sanctified;
An' tuggin' at ye always are the pleasant memories
O' her that was an' is no more—ye can't escape from these.

"Ye've got t' sing an' dance fer years, ye've got t' romp an' play,
An' learn t' love the things ye have by usin' 'em each day;
Even the roses 'round the porch must blossom year by year
Afore they 'come a part o' ye, suggestin' some one dear
Who used t' love 'em long ago, an' trained 'em just t' run
The way they do' so's they would get the early mornin' sun;
Ye've got t' love each brick an' stone from cellar up t' dome,
It takes a heap o' livin' in a house t' make it home."

EDGAR A. GUEST

*   *   *   *

The fine words of Dr. Ferry deserve repeating and reading again and again.

"A house may be destroyed," says Dr. Ferry, "but no power on earth can destroy a true home. Not even death itself can sever the happy relations of hearts joined together in this sacred fellowship.

"I read the other day that the beautiful home of So-and-so had been completely destroyed by fire, but such a statement could not be strictly true; fire cannot destroy a home. It may completely destroy the house that shelters the home, but not the home itself. Many a man has looked upon the smoldering ruins of his house and thought of the priceless things consumed and gone forever, but gathering his loved ones in his arms, he has been able to say, "Thank God, our home is not destroyed"; and taking them, together with all those sacred memories which the ruined house once sheltered, he moves into another house and there reëstablishes his home. The house has been destroyed, but the home is still intact.

It takes more than fire to destroy a true home; there is only one calamity that can ruin a home — the death of love. When love dies, the home is in ruins, and all the material riches, successes, and pleasures of life cannot supply what has been lost.

* * * *

Dr. Payson, meeting an irreligious lady whose husband was trying to serve God, addressed her thus: "Madam, I think your husband is looking upwards, — making some effort to rise above the world towards God and heaven. You must not let him try alone. Whenever I see the husband struggling alone in such efforts, it makes me think of a dove endeavoring to fly upwards while it has one broken wing. It leaps and flutters, and perhaps rises a little way; and then it becomes wearied, and drops back again to the ground. If both wings cooperate, then it mounts easily."

* * * *

The story is told that, it was a source of much trouble to some fishes to see a number of lobsters swimming backwards instead of forwards. They therefore called a meeting. It was determined to open a class for their instruction, which was done, and a number of young lobsters came. The fishes gravely argued, that, if they commenced with the young ones, as they grew up they would learn to swim aright. At first, they did very

well; but afterwards, when they returned home, and
saw their fathers and mothers swimming in the old
way, they soon forgot their lessons. So, many a child
well taught at school is drifted backwards by a *bad
home influence.*

*   *   *   *

That remarkable preacher, F. W. Robertson, truly
said, "Home is the one place in all this world where
hearts are sure of each other. It is the place of confidence. It is the place where we tear off that mask of
guarded and suspicious coldness which the world forces
us to wear in self-defense, and where we pour out the
unreserved communications of full and confiding
hearts. It is the spot where expressions of tenderness
gush out without any sensation of awkwardness, and
without any dread of ridicule."

*   *   *   *

A well-informed writer in the Kilmarnock Standard
states that Thomas Carlyle, not long before his death,
was in conversation with the late Dr. John Brown, and
expressed himself to the following effect: "I am now
an old man, and done with the world. Looking around
me, before and behind, and weighing all as wisely as
I can, it seems to me there is nothing solid to rest on
but the faith which I learned in my old home, and from
my mother's lips."

*   *   *   *

"A man's house," declared Beecher, "should be on
the hill-top of cheerfulness and serenity, so high, that
no shadows rest upon it, and where the morning comes

so early, and the evening tarries so late, that the day
has twice as many golden hours as those of other men.
He is to be pitied whose house is in some valley of grief
between the hills, with the longest night and the short-
est day. Home should be the centre of joy, equatorial
and tropical."

* * * *

"The most miserable homes I have ever known,"
declares J. M. Jones, "have often been those that ought
to have been the happiest. I envied them before I got
to know the whole story. The house was a palace; the
head of the household had worked hard, had made
money. He could command every luxury, and it was
his one pride that everything that money could command was at the disposal of every member of his
home-circle; art had done its best, culture had added
its sweetest ministries; everything there — everything
but the delicate courtesies, the ingenious devices of
love, which are life's most perfect graces."

* * * *

The fine advice of Dr. Phillip should be followed by
all. He rightly contends that it is just as possible to
keep a calm house as a clean house, a cheerful house,
an orderly house, as a furnished house, if the heads set
themselves to do so. Where is the difficulty of con-
sulting each other's weakness, as well as each other's
wants; each other's tempers as well as each other's
health; each other's comfort, as well as each other's
character? Oh! it is by leaving the peace at home to
chance, instead of pursuing it by system, that so many

houses are unhappy. It deserves notice, also, that almost anyone can be courteous and forbearing and patient in a neighbor's house. If anything go wrong, or be out of time, or disagreeable there, it is made the best of, not the worst; even efforts are made to excuse it, and to show that it is not felt; or, if felt, it is attributed to accident, not design; and this is not only easy, but natural, in the house of a friend. I will not, therefore, believe that what is so natural in the house of another is impossible at home; but maintain, without fear, that all the courtesies of social life may be upheld in domestic societies. A husband as willing to be pleased at home, and as anxious to please as in his neighbor's house; and a wife as intent on making things comfortable every day to her family as on set days to her guests, could not fail to make their own home happy. Let us not evade the point of these remarks by recurring to the maxim about allowances for temper. It is worse than folly to refer to our temper, unless we could prove that we gained anything good by giving way to it. Fits of ill-humor punish us quite as much, if not more than those they are vented upon; and it actually requires more effort, and inflicts more pain to give them up, than would be requisite to avoid them.

* * * *

"To be happy at home," remarks Dr. Johnson, "is the ultimate result of all ambition; the end to which every enterprise and labor tends, and of which every desire prompts the prosecution. It is indeed at home that every man must be known by those who would make a just estimate either of his virtue or felicity; for smiles and embroidery are alike occasional, and the mind is often dressed for show in painted honor and fictitious benevolence."

* * * *

"It is a solemn thing to be married," says Beecher, "to have to preach to a congregation from your own loins; to have God put the hand of ordination on you in the birth of your children, and say to you, 'Now art thou a priest unto those whom I have given thee.' If ever the stream of life should flow like crystal water over shining stones, it should be the stream of daily life in the family."

* * * *

The great and good Dr. Goodrich has wisely said that "The fireside is a seminary of infinite importance. Few can receive the honors of a college, but all are graduates of the home. The learning of the university may fade from the recollection, its classic lore may moulder in the halls of memory; but the simple lessons of home, enameled upon the heart of childhood, defy the rust of years, and outlive the more mature but less vivid pictures of after years. So deep, so lasting, indeed, are the impressions of early life, that you often see a man in the imbecility of age holding fresh in his recollection the events of childhood, while all the wide space between that and the present hour is a blasted and forgotten waste. You have perchance seen an old and half-obliterated portrait, and in the attempt to have it cleaned and restored, you may have seen it fade away, while a brighter and more perfect picture, painted beneath, is revealed to view. This portrait, first drawn upon the canvas, is no inapt illustration of youth; and though it may be concealed by some after-design, still the original traits will shine through the outward picture, giving it tone while fresh, and surviving it in decay.

* * * *

"The Presbyterian" received the following *prize answers to the question: "What Is Home?"*

"A world of strife shut out — a world of love shut in."

"Home is the blossom of which Heaven is the fruit."

"The only spot on earth where the faults and failings of fallen humanity are hidden under the mantle of charity."

"The father's kingdom, the children's paradise, the mother's world."

"Where you are treated best and grumble most."

"A little hollow scooped out of the windy hill of the world, where we can be shielded from its cares and annoyances."

* * * *

What makes a home? Four walls of polished stone
Or brick and mortar laid with nicest care?
Nay! Prison walls are made without as fair.
Within—look not within—corruption there
With ignorance and sin defiles the air.

What makes a home? 'Twere better far to roam
Unhoused than have a part in dainty halls,

Where rarest gems of art adorn the walls,
If there's no hearth-fire bright for poorest poor
Who linger in the night without the door.

What makes a home? 'Tis where the weary come
And lay their burdens down, assured of rest.
'Tis where we learn to know our dearest best;
Where little children play, blessing and blest—
Though walls of coarsest clay enwrap the nest.

* * * *

"Blessed is that home," wrote Dr. Talmage, "by which for a whole life-time they have been gathering, until every figure in the carpet, every panel of the door and every casement of the window has a chirography of its own, speaking out something about father or mother, or son or daughter, or friend who was with us awhile. What a sacred place it becomes when one can say: 'In that room such a one was born; in that bed such a one died; in that chair I sat on the night I heard such a one had received a great public honor; by that stool my child knelt for her last evening prayer; here I sat to greet my son as he came back from the sea voyage; that was father's cane; that was mother's rocking chair!' " What a joyful and pathetic congress of reminiscences!

* * * *

There is no spot, or high or low,
    Which darkness visits not at times;
No shelter from the reach of woe,
    In farthest lands of fairest climes.

The tempests shake the stoutest tree,
    And every flow'ret droops in turn:

To mourn is nature's destiny,
    And all that live must live to mourn.

No home so happy, but that pain,
    And grief, and care, the doors will press,
When love's most anxious thoughts are vain,
    More anxious from these helplessness.

And yet, if aught can soften grief,
    'Tis home's sweet influence; if there be
Relief from sorrow, that relief
    Springs from domestic sympathy.

The home that virtue hallows, flings
    Another bliss o'er blessedness;
And e'en to sorrow's children brings
    Or peace to calm, or hope to bless.

                                        John Bowring

* * * *

The angry word suppressed, the taunting thought;
Subduing and subdued, the petty strife
Which clouds the color of domestic life;
The sober comfort, all the peace which springs
From the large aggregate of little things—
On these small cares of daughter, wife, or friend,
The almost sacred joys of home depend.

                                        Hannah More

* * * *

'Mid pleasures and palaces though we may roam,
Still, be it ever so humble, there's no place like home.
A charm from the skies seems to hallow it there,
Which, go through the world, you'll not meet with elsewhere.
    Home, home, sweet home!
    There's no place like home.

An exile from home, pleasure dazzles in vain;
Ah! give me my lowly thatched cottage again.
The birds singing sweetly that come to my call;

Oh, give me sweet peace of mind, dearer than all!
   Home, sweet, sweet home!
   There's no place like home.

                            J. Howard Payne

*　*　*　*

"Home," declares S. Smiles, "is the first and most important school of character. It is there that every human being receives his best moral training or his worst; for it is there that he imbibes those principles of conduct which endure through manhood, and cease only with life. It is a common saying that 'Manners make the man'; and there is a second, 'Mind makes the man'; but truer than either is a third, that 'Home makes the man,' for the home-training includes not only manners and mind, but character. It is mainly in the home that the heart is opened, the habits are formed, the intellect is awakened, and character molded for good or for evil."

*　*　*　*

G. Campbell Morgan says: "My father came into my house soon after I was married, and looked into every room, and then he said to me: 'Yes, it is very nice, but nobody will know, walking through here whether you belong to God or the devil.' I went through and looked at the rooms again, and I thought: 'He is quite right.' So we made up our minds straightway that there should be no room in our house, henceforth, that had not some message, by picture or wall text, for every corner, should tell that we serve the King."

*　*　*　*

To the Greeks the sight of the sea was home. In the

history of the memorable retreat of the ten thousand
Greeks under Xenophon it is said that when they
reached the summit of Mount Theches, from whence
they descried in the distance the tremulously bright
blue of the waters that were to bear them home, in
raptures of joy they instantly shouted out, "The sea!
the sea!" There was one enthusiastic rush, one simul-
taneous cry; they embraced each other and wept, and
in a moment the pang of discomfiture and the toilsome
march of five or six hundred leagues were forgotten
and repaid.

* * * *

The following story contains more truth than fiction,
and may suggest a cause for the lack of devotional life
today. A real estate salesman tried to sell a house to a
newly-married couple. Said the wife: "Why buy a
home? I was born in a hospital, reared in a boarding
school, educated in a college, courted in an automobile,
and married in a church; get my meals in a cafeteria;
live in an apartment; spend my mornings playing golf,
my afternoons playing bridge; in the evenings we dance
or go to the movies; when I'm sick I go to a hospital,
and when I die I shall be buried from an undertaker's.
All we need is a garage with bedroom."

* * * *

The *"Pathfinder"* points out the astounding fact
that of all the children in our orphan asylums, only
five per cent are actually orphans, while sixty-five per
cent have both parents living! Let the advocates of
loose marriage ties figure that out and tell us what

condition we shall be in when people get away alto-
gether from the Bible view of marriage.

*   *   *   *

Whatever you write on the heart of a child,
    No waters can wash it away.
The sands may be shifted when billows are wild
    And the efforts of time may decay.
Some stories may perish, some songs be forgot:
    But this engraven record, time changes it not.
Whatever you write on the heart of a child,
    A story of gladness or care
That heaven has blessed, or that earth has defiled,
    Will linger unchangeably there.
Who writes it has sealed it forever and aye,
    He must answer to God on the great Judgment Day.

*   *   *   *

Chapter IV

CHILDREN

HEAVEN is all around us and angels stand guard over us in our infancy. We should all learn first to appreciate and love God who gave us being; second we should learn to appreciate the Father and Mother who gave us birth; and third the friends who watched over us and cared for us when we were utterly unable to care for ourselves.

We shall never be able to repay or even compensate in any way the love bestowed upon us either by a good gracious God, a much unappreciated loving and marvelous Mother, a Father who slaved and suffered to keep bread and milk on the table and a shelter above the head, or the many kind and unselfish acts of friends all of whom loved us, cared for us, kissed away our cares and sorrows and tears, and tucked us comfortably away in our crib, praying for us when we could not pray for ourselves.

* * * *

"One afternoon I noticed," said Dwight L. Moody, "a young lady at the service whom I knew to be a teacher. After the service I asked her where her class was. 'Oh,' said she, 'I went to the school and found only a little boy, so I came away.' 'Only a little lad,' said I. 'Think of the value of one such soul! The fires of a Reformation may be slumbering in that tow-

40

headed boy! There may be a young Knox, or a Wesley, or a Whitefield in your class.' Christ's advice to Peter was: 'Feed my lambs.' "

*   *   *   *

The sincere and learned Dr. Swing wisely remarked, "We feel free to affirm that no one influence can anywhere be pointed out that will equal the power which Christ has brought to bear upon the republican principles in society. The whole soul of His religion is broad. It is man — man, not rich or poor, not crowned, not chained, but man — who figures in the great Christian drama of life and death. In the religion of Jesus the rich are humiliated if riches be their idol; in the same religion the poor are exalted if they are in the paths of righteousness. Here it was the widow with two mites outranked the Dives of purple and fine linen. Here it was the first began to be last and the last first. Those whom birth, or riches, or force had set up in high places began to sit uneasy on their pedestals of vanity, and slowly up rose Magdalene and all the penitents till forehead of king and forehead of subject found the level of kindred drops. In this transformation scene of the New Testament, children came to the front, and, for the first time on man's world, were made the equals of kings, orators and philosophers. Of such is the kingdom of Heaven."

*   *   *   *

"More and more," says H. C. Potter, "there is growing up a disposition among parents to permit all mat-

ters of religious observance to be with their offspring
mere matters of choice or preference. Your child must
learn French and German and drawing; but he shall
learn his catechism and his Bible lesson and a reverent
observance of Sunday, if he chooses, and not otherwise.
A more dismal and irrational folly it is not easy to
conceive! I do not say that there may not have been
folly in another and opposite direction. I am not un-
mindful that religious teaching has been sometimes
made a dreary and intolerable burden. But surely we
can correct one excess (not, I apprehend, very frequent
or very harmful) without flying straightway into an
opposite and a worse one. And so I plead with you who
are parents to train your children in ways of reverent
familiarity with God's word, God's house, and God's
day. Let them understand that something higher than
your taste or preference makes these things sacred and
binding and constrains you to imbue them with their
spirit. And, that you may do this the more effectually,
give them, I entreat you, that mightiest teaching which
consists in your own consistent and devout example."

*   *   *   *

"Every life," declares the gentle Dr. Jowett, "is the
site of a mine of inconceivable treasure. It is hard to
believe that crusty old Scrooge is the shrine of a sleeping angel. It is hard to believe that Mary Magdalene
is a possible herald of the resurrection morn. But the
assumption of the sleeping angel works, and is a pre-
requisite in all hopeful attempts to unfold the precious-
ness of the individual life. And the assumption must

be accompanied by a sensitive and serious purpose to bring out that buried 'best' which lies in the deep depths of every child."

* * * *

We all know that if we had in youth more models and fewer critics, more caresses and fewer unkindnesses shown us, we all would have been better. Not a few of us have been over-disciplined.

Our natural love for parents has been hurt by the harshness and callousness and insufferable DON'TS of our earthly days, but then we must remember that in most instances it was a sincere desire for our welfare that swung the disciplinary pendulum to the other extreme. Over-anxiety for our good swung the pedulum too far the other way.

Many parents have failed to realize that it is always better to keep children to their duty by a sense of honor and by a reasoning kindness rather than by fear of the rod. Discipline may be too soft and it may be too severe. Better err on the side of kindness and love.

* * * *

Living on the brink of the Grand Canyon of Arizona, there was, a few years ago, an old man who was a luminous character. He lived all alone with himself and the canyon, and he found very good companionship in both. He never tired of watching the effect of the changing lights and shades,—the sunrises and sunsets, and drifting cloud shadows, — on the wonderful coloring of the rocks in the mighty old gorge. He earned his own living; and one day, when he was at work all alone, a company of tourists, at a little distance, heard him laughing very heartily. They hastened to him, asking, "What is the matter? What are you laughing at?" He replied, "Oh, nothing! I was telling myself a funny story." Happy is the man who can be a good companion to himself; who can tell himself entertaining things while he works! This is what we should aim at in the training of children. And in order to attain it in our children, we must attain it in ourselves. We cannot live one kind of life, and train our offspring to another.

* * * *

Michael Fairless in *The Roadmender* tells of a child from the slums who, after listening to the spell of organ music, put up his face to be kissed by the hardened old organ-grinder. The organ-grinder swore at the child and struck him a blow, at which the child ran away in fear. A few days later the organ man met with an accident and lay for days in a hospital, where he was all the time haunted by the memory of that upturned face. As soon as he was well again he went in search of the child that tried to kiss him, playing the tunes which always drew the children out of the alleys to his organ. He never found the child whom he had repelled, but in his loving search for him he became kind and gentle, loving and noble in spirit, and says of him, "He saw the face of a little child and looked on God." It is exactly what would happen to anyone who recovered the child spirit and it is what has happened to many of us.

*   *   *   *

What a vast difference wise child-nurture would have made in Byron's life! Schopenhauer had reference to this when he said, after being told that he had been sitting next to the poet's mother, Lady Byron, at dinner: "I wish I had known it at the time; I should have liked to be rude to her."

*   *   *   *

Bishop William Taylor was accustomed to say: "There are no heathen children. Little children the wide world around are of the kingdom." There is a picture of him standing beside a little Negro girl in Africa, for whose education he had become responsible. Years afterward a companion picture appeared with him standing beside a fine dignified colored woman, showing what Christian education in the wilds of Africa had done for the little Negro child. "No heathen children!" The church's task is to get hold of them in time to prevent their being misled by the influences that surround them and destroy their natural capacity for a Christian life. Perhaps this is what Christ meant when he said of the babies, "Of such is the kingdom of heaven." As children in years, or redeemed to child-likeness in later life, they belong in the kingdom because they possess the childlike qualities.

*   *   *   *

The brilliant and benign John Willis Baer tells the following story:

"Sitting back of me in a train the other day were a

mother and her promising boy. The conductor had punched the mother's ticket, and as a ticket had not been provided for the lad, the conductor, looking at the boy, politely said, 'is your boy under five, madam?'

" 'Yes,' was the prompt reply.

"The conductor moved on, and then I heard the youngster say, 'Why, mamma, I am past six.'

"Instantly, with frowning face and a countenance blazing with wrath, the mother said: 'Don't ever contradict me again. I know what I am saying. If the conductor had heard you say that, he would have made me pay half-fare for you. Don't ever say again on the train that you are past six. If you do, I'll whip you when we get home.'

"The boy was still and thoughtful for a moment. Then I heard him say, 'But, mamma, I *am* past six.' A slap followed; the child cried; the mother looked like a tempest; and I fairly boiled with indignation.

"It is just an incident on a railroad train, yet possibly one that will be more harmful to a boy morally than an ordinary railroad accident might have been to him physically. One such experience in a boy's life may mar his whole career. Then think of the mother's personal sins. She lied to the conductor; she lied to her own boy; she cheated the railroad; she abused the child. And all that to save one dollar and twenty-five cents, the price of a half-fare ticket from New York to Philadelphia. May God pity the boy and forgive the mother."

* * * *

A suggestion as to the value of Christian nurture in

Sabbath-school work is found in the remark made by that very successful lay missionary among the depraved classes in New York City, Jerry McAuley. He made the statement more than once, that he never knew a man permanently converted unless he had a good mother. We are not called upon to accept that remark as stating a rule in the history of conversions. But that Jerry McAuley should have made it as a result of close observation of his converts is a sufficient reason why Sabbath-school officers and teachers should give close attention to the scholars who have good mothers.

* * * *

For those who may be feeling the pinch of poverty we include the following lines by May Riley Smith:

> Across in my neighbor's window,
>   With its folds of satin and lace,
> I see, with its crown of ringlets,
>   A baby's innocent face.
> The throngs in the street look upward,
>   And every one, grave and gay,
> Has a nod and smile for the baby
>   In the mansion over the way.
>
> Just here in my cottage window,
>   His chin in his dimpled hands,
> And a patch on his faded apron,
>   The child that I live for stands.
> He has kept my heart from breaking
>   For many a weary day;
> And his face is as pure and handsome
>   As the baby over the way.

Sometimes, when we sit together,
    My grave little man of three
Sore vexes me with the question:
    "Does God, up in Heaven, like me?"
And I say: "Yes—yes, my darling!"
    Though I almost answer "nay,"
As I see the nursery candles
    In the mansion over the way.

And oft when I draw the stockings
    From the little tired feet,
And loosen the clumsy garments
    From his limbs, so round and sweet,
I grow too bitter for singing,
    My heart too heavy to pray,
As I think of the dainty raiment
    Of the baby over the way.

O God in Heaven, forgive me
    For all I have thought and said:
My envious heart is humbled—
    My neighbor's baby is dead!
I saw the little white coffin
    As they carried it out today,
And the heart of a mother is breaking
    In the mansion over the way.

The light is fair in my window,
    The flowers bloom at my door;
My boy is chasing the sunbeams
    That dance on the cottage floor.
The roses of health are crowning
    My darling's forehead today;
But the baby is gone from the window
    Of the mansion over the way.

*   *   *   *

The Rev. Moses Browne had twelve children. On one remarking to him, "Sir, you have just as many children as Jacob," he replied, "Yes; and I have Jacob's God to provide for them."

* * * *

Children should be treated by parents as God treats parents. Children should be loved, honored and respected and they should in turn love, honor and respect others.

It is no slight thing to be loved by a child and it is no small matter to be slighted or shunned by a child. Every true lover of God loves little children. Infinite wrongs have been inflicted on childhood by loveless, hardboiled disciplinarians. Rods, dark rooms, neglectful mothers, selfish pre-occupied fathers, and scolding, frowning school masters and mistresses should be the very last resources in the correcting of a tender and sensitive child. Any bully can crush the spirit and still the cry of a baby. It takes real love and a real man and a noble woman to bear with them and patiently seek to discover the secret of their discomfort.

* * * *

A little boy asked his mother which of the characters in *Pilgrim's Progress* she liked best. She replied, "Christian, of course; he is the hero of the story." Her son said, "I don't, mother; I like Christiana best, for when Christian went on his pilgrimage he started alone, but when Christiana went she took the children with her."

* * * *

Gypsy Smith once said, "On four English-speaking

continents I have been for a quarter of a century trying to deal with men and women and children, and, oh, how many boys and girls have come to me and said, when life had become ruined for them, "Ah, Mr. Smith! my life would have been different if my father had prayed, but I have not a praying father."

* * * *

A young lady was talking about her brother, who had just entered the medical profession. She confessed that he was not much of a physician yet, but he had got far enough along to doctor babies! Of course she thought he was successful in that line. Whether the undertakers and mothers agreed in the verdict is not recorded. Little lives go out so quickly that of all people babies need the best professional skill. The application to the Sunday school is obvious. The primary department needs and is entitled to the best teachers. Those little people are impressible. They believe what is told them. Thoughts of God, of Christ, of eternity, of right and wrong, move them more quickly and abide longer in their fresh souls than in the more hardened natures of adults. Look out for your infant school first, last and all the time.

* * * *

"Follow me," says a recent traveler in Palestine, "into the grove, and I will show you what may have suggested the comparison. Here we have hit upon a beautiful illustration. This aged and decayed tree is surrounded, as you see, by several young and thrifty shoots, which spring from the roots of the venerable parent. They seem to uphold, protect, and embrace it. We may even fancy that they now bear that load of fruit which would otherwise be demanded of the feeble parent. Thus do good and affectionate children gather round the table of the righteous. Each contributes something to the common wealth and welfare of the whole,—a beautiful sight, with which may God refresh the eyes of every friend of mine!"

* * * *

Kindness, reason and persuasion should always be tried before brute force. The sugar plum may prevail where the rod may fail.

"As for ourselves," once confessed Beecher, "we tried the rod on our own children, but are now trying the sugar-plum with our grandchildren. Thus far, our success is remarkable. Family government has risen in popularity. Children cry for it. Our children used to look with aversion on the spot where we locked up the switch; but now there is not in the whole house a place so favorite as the drawer where is stored the sweet moral suasion. Good conduct thrives; obedience is at a premium; the will is broken; the children are governed without knowing it. Blessings on sugar-plums!"

* * * *

That master of Simile and Hyperbole, Dr. Cawdray, once wisely said, "As Alexander the Great attained to have such a puissant army, whereby he conquered the world, by having children born and brought up in his camp, whereby they became so well acquainted and exercised with weapons from their swaddling-clothes, that they looked for no other wealth or country but to fight: even so, if thou wouldst have thy children either to do great matters, or to live honestly by their own virtuous endeavors, thou must acquaint them with painstaking in their youth, and so to bring them up in the nurture and admonition of the Lord."

*   *   *   *

There is a striking story of a certain missionary who was sent for, on one occasion, to go to a little village in an out-of-the-way corner of India to baptize and receive into church fellowship seventy adult converts from Hinduism. A boy about fifteen years of age came forward. "What, my boy! do you want to join the church?" "Yes, sir."

On the score of his youth he urged the lad to wait until his return in six months.

Then all the people said, "Why, sir, it is he that has taught us all that we know about Jesus Christ." And so it turned out to be. This was the little minister of the little church, the honored instrument in the hand of God for saving all the rest for Jesus Christ.

*   *   *   *

A child is undefiled by a wicked world, unvexed as yet by its many injustices and unwearied by its many pleasures. A sincere effort should be made to mold its brain cells into channels of holiness, unselfishness and usefulness. Its love nature should be carefully and patiently protected.

*   *   *   *

There are 10,000 boys in the reform schools of this country under seventeen years of age. Most of the criminals of this country are under twenty. Jonathan Edwards was only eleven when he was converted. Wesley and Luther were about the same age, and Spurgeon was fourteen. You cannot tell what the boy may become. Do not be afraid to work for him. A bishop once remarked: "If the Church neglects the children, the devil will not." There is much truth there, for the devil neglects not for a single minute. Never give a boy up, no matter how bad you may think him. Wild boys often make the best men.

* * * *

That intellectual giant, Dr. Tillotson, was born in 1630 and died in 1694. Before his death he gave this advice to parents.

"Consider," he said, "what a sad inheritance you have conveyed to your children. You have transmitted to them corrupt and depraved natures, evil and vicious inclinations: you have begotten them in your own image and likeness, so that by nature they are children of wrath. Now, methinks, parents that have a due sense of this should be very solicitous, by the best means they can use, to free them from that curse; by endeavoring to correct those perverse dispositions, and cursed inclinations, which they have transmitted to them. Surely you ought to do all you can to repair that broken estate which from you is descended upon them.

When a man hath by treason tainted his blood and

forfeited his estate, with what grief and regret doth
he look upon his children, and think of the injury he
hath done to them by his fault; and how solicitous is
he, before he die, to petition the king for favor to his
children; how earnestly doth he charge his friends to
be careful of them and kind to them; that by these
means he may make the best reparation he can of their
fortune which hath been ruined by his fault.

And have parents such a tenderness for their children, in reference to their estate and condition in this
world; and have they none for the good estate of their
souls and their eternal condition in another world?
If you are sensible that their blood is tainted, and that
their best fortunes are ruined by your sad misfortune,
why do you not bestir yourselves for the repairing of
God's image in them? Why do you not travail in birth
till Christ be formed in them? Why do you not pray
earnestly to God, and give Him no rest, who hath
reprieved you that He would extend His grace to them
also, and grant them the blessings of His new covenant?

* * * *

A rich Crow Indian in Montana, named "White
Arm," had in some way gotten hold of the true idea
of "possessions." A missionary needed some land to
establish a school farm to teach the little Indians how
to work as well as pray. He applied to the government agent and found all the land thereabouts had
been allotted to the Indians. "Take my land," said
"White Arm." He gave them one hundred and sixty
acres. Another missionary, on arriving in the place,

happened to say, "I wish I had my wife and children here!" "Why don't you?" asked "White Arm." Because I have no place to put them." "Take my house," said "White Arm." In spite of the missionary's protest he moved out into a tent and left his house empty and open, so that the missionary could not refuse to take it. Afterward he said that he did all for the children of his tribe, that the missionary might lead them and their parents to the true God.

* * * *

The child's influence for good has been aptly set forth by Dr. C. S. Robinson.

"Children are not apt," says Robinson, "to remember how much good they can do merely with words they can speak. Sometimes I think they can do even more than men and women; for nobody is half as likely to be angry with a child for telling him what he ought not to do as he would, perhaps, be with a minister or some older person. I have known the hardest sort of people to be quite kind and thoughtful when rebuked by those who were too small for them to strike or curse for being faithful.

"Not long ago, I read, there was a Highland boy sitting on the door-stone, with some half-dozen others. They were singing Sunday-school hymns. Along came a half-drunken man, who said with an awful oath, 'Does your master teach you nothing better than these silly songs?' When up spoke this sharp little fellow, six years old: 'Why, yes, sir. He teaches us it is wicked for any one to *swear!*' The man hurried on silently, as if he were ashamed; and afterwards told how he had become a better man because of the rebuke the child gave him.

"There was a great and good man lecturing in London; and he happened to say: 'Everybody has influence; even that little girl.' And as he said this, he pointed to a child sitting on her father's knee. 'That is true,' said the man, right out in the meeting. Afterward he waited to make an apology for the interruption. 'I could not help speaking,' he said. 'I used to be a drunkard, and this little girl of mine pleaded with me to stop going to the ale-house. I was angry, and knocked her down. But she got up and came straight to me, saying: ' 'Twasn't you, father, but the rum, that struck me.' And I felt so sorry that I never went again. This little child is my very best friend in the world."

*   *   *   *

Parents should remember that children also have their rights, and children should always bear in mind that Mother and Father always know best what is good in both the present and the future. If a child can be brought to tears by being shown the seriousness of an offense such a child needs no rod and should be given no other chastisement. Parents should threaten less and forbear a little more. Better to break a promise than to administer unjust, unfair and unmerciful punishment, for children do not forget. A child, full of hope, overflowing with curiosity, and conscious of no guile is God's gift to a home.

*   *   *   *

In twenty-five years of ministry and having taken into membership in one year some fifty children, the writer has never once had cause to regret his practice of encouraging child conversion and then their acceptance into full membership of the church.

I have, during the past year, received forty or fifty children into church-membership. Among those I have had at any time to exclude from church-fellowship, out of a church of several hundred members, I have never had to exclude a single one who was received while yet a child. Teachers and superintendents should not merely believe in the possibility of early conversion, but in the frequency of it.

* * * *

Prof. Jacob R. Street has truly said, "Adolescence is peculiarly the time of criminality. Statistics show that the greater number of arrests occur during adolescence. It is also the time of strong religious impulses. The life oftentimes seems to vacillate between these two potencies. Some morning the child wakes up to find himself capable of committing crimes he never dreamed of before. Some morning he finds in himself a spiritual consciousness. These are the natural development, and the teacher and the parent should look forward to this period with prescience, fully assured that they have the golden privilege of directing the incompetent feet of youth away from the dalliant path of vice into the highway of holiness. It is estimated that the sun never shines without some boy or girl in these United States takes his or her own life, driven

thereto by the emotional potency peculiar to this age.
And the most depressing thought is that the destruc-
tive volcano slumbering in the youth is set into erup-
tion by the thoughtless word or deed of a teacher or
parent."

*   *   *   *

The least impressions received in infancy have consequences tremendously important, far-reaching and
eternal. The waters of a river may be easily turned
in its beginning and it is the same with the mind of a
little child. Napoleon, Hitler, Stalin, Mussolini were
once children. What miseries might have been saved
the world of mankind if some kind and tender hand
had been laid upon them in childhood and watched
lovingly and patiently over them in youth. In the
city of Bellaire, Ohio, there is a grave. In the grave
is the charred body of a young mother. She was
burned to a crisp in an electric chair in the State of
Pennsylvania. She took part in the murder of a state
trooper. On the witness stand she testified that never
once in all her life had she ever been invited by
anyone either to Sunday School or Church. Bellaire
is a city of churches. The young child, the growing
girl, the loving maid, the unfortunate wife, the young
mother was never once by anyone invited to God,
Christ, the Church or to Sunday School. What a reckoning day for someone.

*   *   *   *

A young prince, whose mind had learned in some
degree to value religious truth, asked his tutor to give

him suitable instruction, that he might be prepared for death. "Plenty of time for that when you are older," was the reply. "No!" said the prince, "I have been to the church-yard and measured the graves; and there are many *shorter* than I am."

* * * *

We must warn parents against the vicious habit of making a groove and then compelling a child to walk in it. That which succeeds in one instance will miserably fail in another.

"Many children," declared Beecher, "grow up like plants under bell-glasses. They are surrounded only by artificial and prepared influences. They are house-bred, room-bred, nurse-bred, mother-bred, — every thing but *self-bred*. The object of training is to teach the child to take care of himself: but many parents use their children only as a kind of spool on which to reel off their own experience; and they are bound and corded until they perish by inanity, or break all bonds and cords, and rush to ruin by re-action."

* * * *

Every child is an apostle of love, cheer and promise. What a calamity to destroy them either suddenly by dislike or slowly by neglect.

Destinies are decided in the cradle and the day nursery — destinies not only of individuals, but of states and nations. The children of today are the architects of tomorrow. Oh! why not seek to soften and tenderize them for the tasks ahead.

Like a mirror children reflect after life the images

first presented to them. "Train up a child in the way" ordered the wise man in Proverbs 22:6. Ah! but training takes time, patience and perseverance, whereas the rod, the slap, the sting, the don't do that and don't do the other, the kick, the punch and the jerk is easier for us. Because of this the jails are filled with once fine little fellows and the potters field overflowing with once pure and gentle girls.

* * * *

It is said of that German schoolmaster John Trebonius, the instructor of Martin Luther, that he always appeared before his boys with uncovered head. "Who can tell," said he "what may yet rise up amid these youths? There may be among them those who shall be learned doctors, sage legislators, nay, princes of the empire." Even then there was among them that "solitary monk that shook the world."

* * * *

A child is a rose with its leaves as yet unfolded and unblasted. What an opportunity for some kind heart and hand! A child is tomorrow's father or mother, tomorrow's President or pauper, slouch or senator. What an opportunity for some preacher or teacher!

The child of today is the s o c i e t y of the future. What a tragedy to kill its conscience or hurt its little tender heart. We all know that as the twig is bent the tree will grow, and yet we callously neglect the twig. God have mercy upon us all. Shall we everlastingly and purposefully forget that as certain as the smallest planets are nearer the sun so the smallest child needs to be brought nearest and closest to God.

* * * *

"Discipline" writes Dr. James, "should respect each child in particular according to his disposition. In the same family there may be a variety of tempers, which will require a varied method of treatment, in addition to the general principles of education which will apply alike to all minds. And therefore, as the farmer consults the nature of his land, adapting the seed to the soil; and as the physician studies the constitution of his patient, suiting the remedy to the disease; so ought every parent to study the dispositions of all his children, that he may adapt his discipline to the particularities of their respective tempers."

* * * *

Dr. Henry Kulp Ober tells the story of a little fellow who climbed into his mother's lap, put his chubby arms around her neck and eagerly asked, "Please explain the picture on the parlor wall to me." The mother answered gently, "Certainly." The picture showed a woman coming down the path, preceded by a group of happy little girls casting bouquets into her pathway. The mother said, "That is a beautiful picture. The lady is a good mother and a great teacher and these little girls have learned to love her. To show their love for her they have filled their baskets with flowers and are throwing them gently into her pathway." "Oh, I see!" He planted a few kisses on her cheek, slipped from her lap, and ran off to play.

Two days later the same mother came into the same

parlor and found her fine brussels carpet literally covered with rose petals from door to sofa. A flood of anger overcame her — "Father, forgive us for such blunders." She called in a stern voice and asked a stinging question. Without listening for the answer she pronounced the sentence, sending him upstairs into a dark closet for an hour as punishment. "Imagine," said she, "my fine brussels carpet." Then tried to calm herself by saying, "He will soon be asleep."

Coming to the foot of the stairway near the end of the hour she heard sobs. She rushed there and upon opening the closet door heard what she might have heard before, had she listened. In broken sobs came these words, "I can't understand why my mamma can't understand me." When he beheld her he cried all the harder as he rushed into her arms and said, "Mother, did you not tell me the other day that the little girls in the picture on the parlor wall loved that good mother so much and that they strewed flowers in her path to show their love? I went into the yard under the rose bushes and picked up the petals by the handfuls and strewed them from the door of the parlor to the sofa where you and I sat, to show how much I loved you. Why, then, did you punish me? Where was I wrong?"

That mother had crushed with one sentence the finest flower that can bloom in a child's heart. Did not motive determine the value of his act? Who has sense keen enough to measure the outcome of so sweet a sentiment crystallized into conduct and thus becom-

ing a part of character? God f o r g i v e us for such
blindness.

* * * *

The author of the following lines is unknown.

A woman sat by the hearthside place,
Reading a book with a pleasant face,
'Til a child came up and jogged her knee,
Saying, "Put it down and take me."
    The mother slapped the curly head,
    As she rather gruffly said,
"A great deal of Christ's life I must know
To teach you how you should go."
    That child went to bed to cry
    And denounce religion by and by.

A woman sat by the hearthside place,
Reading a book with a pleasant face,
'Til a child came up and jogged her knee,
Saying, "Put it down and take me."
    The mother smiled and stroked his little head,
    And with compassion sweetly said,
"I guess I never will get it fully read.
I shall try into my child instill
Love and the Master's will."
    That child went to bed without a sigh
    And will love religion by and by.

* * * *

The great and good Dr. Gurnall was born in 1617.
Speaking upon the subject of Religious Training,
Gurnall grandly remarked, "Our children are not born
with Bibles in their heads or hearts. And who ought
to be the instructor, if not the parent? yea, who will
do it with such natural affection? As I have heard
sometimes a mother say in other respects, Who can

take such pains with my child, and be so careful as
myself that am its mother." Bloody parents then they
are, who acquaint not their children with God or His
Word; what do they but put them under a necessity
of perishing, if God stir not up some to show more
mercy than themselves to them? Is it any wonder to
hear that ship to be sunk or dashed upon the rock
which was put to sea without chart or compass? no
more it is they should ingulf themselves in sin and
perdition that are thrust forth into the world (which
is a sea of temptation) without the knowledge of God,
or their duty to Him."

* * * *

Maclaren, the Expositor of Scripture, reminds us
that, "It is the law of human nature that, when it is
beginning to grow, it shall be soft as wax to receive
all kinds of impressions, and then that it shall gradually stiffen and become hard as adamant to retain
them. The rock was once all fluid and plastic, and
gradually it cools down into hardness. If a finger-dint
had been put upon it in the early time, it would have
left a mark that all the forces of the world could not
make, nor can obliterate now. In our great museums
you see stone slabs with the marks of rain that fell
hundreds of years before Adam lived; and the foot-
print of some wild bird that passed across the beach
in those old, old times. The passing shower and the
light foot left their prints on the soft sediment; then
ages went on, and it has hardened into stone; and
there they remain and will remain for evermore. That

is like a man's spirit; in the childish days so soft, so susceptible to all impressions, so joyous to receive new ideas, treasuring them all up, gathering them all into itself, retaining them all forever. And then, as years go on, habit, the growth of the soul into steadiness and power, and many other reasons beside, gradually make us less and less capable of being profoundly and permanently influenced by anything outside us; so that the process from childhood to manhood is a process of getting less impressible.

O mothers, so weary, discouraged,
    Worn out with the cares of the day,
You often grow cross and impatient,
    Complain of the noise and the play;
For the day brings so many vexations,
    So many things going amiss;
But mothers, whatever may vex you,
    Send the children to bed with a kiss!

The dear little feet wander often,
    Perhaps, from the pathway of right,
The dear little hands find new mischief
    To try you from morning till night;
But think of the desolate mothers
    Who'd give all the world for your bliss,
And, as thanks for your infinite blessings,
    Send the children to bed with a kiss!

For some day their noise will not vex you,
    The silence will hurt you far more;
You will long for their sweet childish voices,
    For a sweet childish face at the door;
And to press a child's face to your bosom,
    You'd give all the world for just this!
For the comfort 'twill bring you in sorrow,
    Send the children to bed with a kiss!

* * * *

"Tell me not of the trim, precisely-arranged homes where there are no children," declared the much loved Mary Howitt, " 'where,' as the good Germans have it, 'the fly-traps always hang straight on the wall'; tell me not of the never-disturbed nights and days, of the tranquil, unanxious hearts, where children are not! I care not for these things. God sends children for another purpose than merely to keep up the race: — to enlarge our hearts, to make us unselfish, and full of kindly sympathies and affections; to give our souls higher aims, and to call out all our faculties to extended enterprise and exertion; to bring round our fireside bright faces and happy smiles, and loving, tender hearts. My soul blesses the Great Father every day, that He has gladdened the earth with little children."

* * * *

A father is as it were a prince and a judge in his family: there he gives laws, and inflicts censures and punishments upon offenders. But how misbecoming a thing would it be to see a judge in choler pass sentence upon a man? It is the same thing to see a father in the heat and fury of his passion correct his child. If a father could but see himself in this mood, and how ill his passion becomes him, instead of being angry with his child, he would be out of patience with himself.

* * * *

Children are never happy if idle and it is a crime to neglect them for hours leaving them to entertain themselves. Here is one sure way to make ill looking and ill tempered children out of them. The man who dislikes the laughs and cries of a little child will bear watching. The woman who would rather pet a poodle than a pretty babe is a monstrosity.

* * * *

The following story is repeated by Dr. Elihu Burritt.

"Yes, they are good boys," I once heard a kind father say; "I talk to them very much, but do not like to beat my children — the world will beat them." It was a beautiful thought, though not elegantly expressed. Yes: there is not one child in the circle round the table, healthful and happy as they look now, on whose head, if long enough spared, the storm will not beat. Adversity may wither them, sickness may fade, a cold world may frown on them, but amidst all let memory carry them back to a home where the law of kindness reigned, where the mother's reproving eye was moistened with a tear, and the father frowned "more in sorrow than in anger."

* * * *

While the Rev. Mr. Chambers was once addressing a temperance meeting in Philadelphia, a man who had been occupying a seat in a distant part of the room, arose with a little boy in his arms, scarce six years old, and came forward to the speaker's stand; all gave way for him. He placed his child on the stand, and while the tears were running fast down his cheeks, and with trembling accents, addressed the speaker: "My little boy said to me, 'Father, do not drink any more!' Gentlemen, I have taken my last drink." The effect produced upon the audience beggars all description. The speaker and the whole audience were bathed in tears;

and such was the good effects of this example, that *seventeen* others came forward and signed the PLEDGE!

*   *   *   *

One of the stories about the Knights of the Round Table is that of a dwarf remarkable for his smallness and deformity, who used to go around the court of King Arthur, carrying a drawn sword, and imploring the knights one after another to take it and cut off his head. He was a poor wretch, apparently of no value in the world; but he had never done anybody any harm, and so they naturally declined to gratify what seemed his crazed desire. At last he came to Sir Gawain, as noble and true a knight as ever breathed, and said, "Gawain, do you love me?" "Why yes," replied the knight, "you know that I love you, and what would you have me to do for you to show my love?" "I would have you take this sword, and with it cut off my head," was the answer. Sir Gawain, like all the others, shrank from such a deed. But there was something in the dwarf's tone so imploring that he finally consented, and with a single blow cleft the head clear of the body, and down the two parts fell prone to the earth. But, lo! as soon as the earth was touched, out of the little deformed dwarf there sprang up a tall and graceful knight, full of all strength and goodness, who had been imprisoned in it many years before by a great magician's skill, and who from that hour went forth to do God and the world a noble service. And in this same way the man is potentially in the boy, waiting to be liberated.

*   *   *   *

The Rev. Mr. Solomon Carpenter held a religious meeting in Sussex county, Mass., at the house of a man who was addicted to swearing, and the minister took occasion to reprove this and other vices. A little girl belonging to the family withdrew, and placed herself behind the door, and began to weep very bitterly. Her father particularly asked her the cause of this, and she told him she was afraid he would go to hell on account of his swearing. He at length promised her that if she would refrain from weeping he would never swear any more. The child was now quiet, and in an ecstacy of joy afterwards told her mother of the promise she had obtained from her father. The unexpected reproof the father had thus received from his daughter was lastingly impressed on his mind; he became a humble penitent, and lived to be a shining light in the Christian community with which he was afterwards connected.

* * * *

Dr. Hillis tells the story that, a century ago an English deist, calling upon Coleridge, inveighed bitterly against the rigid instruction in Christian homes. "Consider," said he, "the helplessness of a little child. Before it has wisdom or judgment to decide for itself it is prejudiced in favor of Christianity. How selfish is the parent who stamps his religious ideas into a child's receptive nature, as a molder stamps the hot iron with his model. I shall prejudice my children neither for Christianity nor for Buddhism nor for atheism, but allow them to wait for their mature years.

Then they can open the question and decide for themselves." Later the poet led his atheistic acquaintance into the garden. Suddenly he explained: "How selfish is the gardener who ruthlessly stamps his prejudice in favor of roses and violets and strawberries into a receptive gardenbed. The time was when in April I pulled up the young weeds, the parsley, and thistle, and planted the garden-beds out with vegetables and flowers. Now I have decided to permit the garden to go until September. Then the black clods can choose for themselves between cockleberries and currants and strawberries."

* * * *

There was an abbot who desired a piece of ground that lay conveniently for him. The owner refused to sell it, yet, with much persuasion, was contented to let it. The abbot hired it for his rent, and covenanted only to farm it with one crop. He had his bargain, and sowed it with acorns, — a crop that lasted three hundred years. Thus Satan begs but for the first crop. Let him sow thy youth with acorns: they will grow up with thy years to sturdy oaks, so big-bulked and deep-rooted, that they shall last all thy life.

* * * *

We should everlastingly bear in mind that while a child by nature's kindly law may be pleased with a rattle and tickled by a straw it is also true that they may also be ruined by a look, killed by a kick, knocked senseless by a slap, and turned into hooligans by unkindness and hard harsh words. Torn jackets are

soon mended, dirty dresses are soon washed, broken
dishes are easily replaced but a bruised, hurt or broken
heart is not so easily healed. Where is the man whose
childhood was blessed with kindness, caresses and
kisses? In him you will find a heart that may be
touched to gentle issues and influenced for Christ and
holiness.

Oh, to appreciate the privilege of loving and leading
that little life before he is sent out to drag heavy
artillery along the dusty and dirty, blood stained high-
ways of earth.

*   *   *   *

"In dibbling beans," says Spurgeon, "the old practice was to put three in each hole: one for the worm,
one for the crow, and one to live and produce the crop.
In teaching children, we must give line upon line, and
precept upon precept, repeating the truth which we
would inculcate, till it becomes impossible for the child
to forget it. We may well give the lesson once expect-
ing the child's frail memory to lose it; twice, reckoning
that the devil, like an ill bird, will steal it; thrice,
hoping that it will take root downward, and bring
forth fruit upward to the glory of God."

*   *   *   *

The impressions of childhood, says another writer,
are proverbially the most indelible. The mind of man
is like one of those ancient manuscripts that are covered with successive layers of writing, of which the
last alone is visible; but the application of a chemical
test reveals all the rest. In like manner, the human

mind is covered with innumerable layers of imperish-
able memories. We speak of forgetfulness; but, in
truth, we forget nothing — at least, in the sense of
its passing entirely from the mind. Thus we find in
the case of very old people, that, while the events of
the present make scarcely any impression at all on the
memory, the reminiscences of childhood come trooping
back in all the vivid freshness of youth.

* * * *

The learned Lamartine declared that, the future
state of the child depends in a great measure upon
the home in which he is born. His soul is nourished
and grows, above all, by the impressions which are
there left upon his memory. My father gave me the
example of a sincerity carried even to scrupulousness;
my mother, of a goodness rising to devotion the most
heroic. . . I drank deep from my mother's mind; I
read through her eyes; I felt through her impressions;
I lived through her life.

* * * *

"Some of you may remember," says F. G. Peabody,
"at the two hundred and fiftieth anniversary of our
College, how the students marched in a great torch-
light procession, with many original transparencies
and banners, and how the freshman class, then only a
month old as students, carried at their head this motto:
'The University has been waiting two hundred and fifty
years for us.' That was very amusing; but to any one
who could read the deeper facts of the University the
motto conveyed a profound and solemn truth. All this

great, historic, institutional life had been indeed slowly evolved for the sake of these newly-arrived light-hearted boys, and now on their conduct were resting the destinies of the future, and out of their wise uses of their student life were to come our later blessings."

* * * *

Doctor Potter tells the story of a young man who stood at the bar of a court of justice to be sentenced for forgery. The judge had known him from a child, for his father had been a famous legal light and his work on the Law of Trusts was the most exhaustive work on the subject in existence. "Do you remember your father," asked the judge sternly, "that father whom you have disgraced?" The prisoner answered: "I remember him perfectly. When I went to him for advice or companionship, he would look up from his book on the 'Law of Trusts' and say, 'Run away, boy, I am busy.' My father finished his book, and here I am." The great lawyer had neglected his own trust with awful results.

* * * *

As certain as soft wax takes the stamp of the seal so the minds of little children receive the instruction and examples imprinted upon them.

Jesus recognized the growing possibilities of little children. Christ was the first great teacher among men to show a genuine loving and understanding sympathy for childhood and may we never forget that "of such is the kingdom of heaven." To offend such, to harm such, to hurt such, to bend such in a wrong

direction is an affront against God, Christ and High
Heaven.

*   *   *   *

A farmer decided to remove an old beech-tree which
grew on his farm. The wood-cutter noticed on the
bark of the tree some curious marks looking like the
letters J. L., roughly cut, and below them some orna-
mental design. After the tree had been cut down and
was being separated into lengths he was startled to
find on the hard, dry wood at the core of the tree,
directly opposite the place on the bark where he had
noticed the marks, the clearly cut letters J. L., on a
dark background, and below them an anchor. On in-
quiries being made, it was found that the letters were
the initials of a sailor named John Leland, who, in an
idle hour, had cut them on the beech-tree when it was
young. There were thirty-seven rings between the
letters and the bark of the tree, and the woodsman
said that each ring represented one year's growth of
the tree. He inferred that the letters must have been
cut in the year 1853, and his belief was confirmed
when he learned that it was in that year that the
sailor had spent some time in that neighborhood. Thus
the inscription had not only remained in the place
where it was cut at first, but as each year added to
the growth of the tree, the letters still appeared on
the surface, scarcely legible there, it is true, but perfectly clear at the core. It is so with human character.
Many an old man, in spite of the rough usage of the
world and the scars of time and trouble, bears upon

his walk and conversation the marks of the hand-writing which in his youth God put in his heart.

* * * *

No photographic plate on earth is so exquisitively sensitive as is a child to catch and retain impressions.

This scribe pays homage to his marvelous mother who welcomed him into the world and to a father to whom he largely owes a strong body and reasonably sound mind.

* * * *

"In the home of a pious farmer," says Dr. W. W. Landrum, "there hung the well-known motto: 'But as for me and my house, we will serve the Lord.' The motto meant something in that house, for the farmer prayed daily that all might truly serve the Lord. The last clause fitted all the house except the oldest son, who persistently refused to accept Christ. One day the father and son were alone in the room where the motto hung. The father said, 'My dear Henry, I can not and will not be a liar any longer. You, who belong to my house, do not want to serve the Lord. Therefore I must add the words "except Henry"; it hurts me to do it, but I must be true.' The thought so impressed the boy that he gave himself to Christ."

* * * *

A pretty story is told of Leonardo da Vinci's boy-hood. The little fellow was accustomed to buy such caged birds as he saw exposed for sale on the streets of Florence that he might set them free. The little Leonardo early learned the lesson that there is more

genuine pleasure in a good act than in a good possession. There are, in the path in which each of us walk,
many caged birds which we can set free. Of all keys
to unlock the prison captives sympathy is the best. A
kind word of praise, a hearty expression of good-will,
a little help offered at the right time — none of these
things cost much, but each may make the difference,
to many a sad heart, between joy and sorrow.

* * * *

"God bless the dear children!" once declared the
silver tongued Talmage. "What would our homes be
without them! We may have done much for them.
They have done more for us. What a salve for a
wounded heart there is in the soft palm of a child's
hand. Did harp or flute ever have such music as there
is in a child's 'good-night.' From our coarse, rough
life, the angels of God are often driven back; but who
comes into the nursery without feeling that angels are
hovering around.

"On one of the Lake steamers there was a father
and two daughters journeying. They seemed extremely
poor. A benevolent gentleman stepped up to the poor
man, to proffer some form of relief, and said, 'You
seem to be very poor, sir.' 'Poor, sir!' replied the man,
'if there's a poorer man than me a troublin' the world,
God pity both of us!' 'I will take one of your children,
and adopt it, if you say so. I think it would be a
great relief to you.' 'A *what?*' said the poor man. 'A
relief! Would it be a relief to have the hands chopped
off from the body, or the heart torn from the breast?

A relief, indeed! God be good to us! What do you mean, sir?"

* * * *

Once there was at Oxford University a little boot-black named George. He was bright and active. The boys liked him very much. At length one of them said: "A boy who can black shoes well can study well." The other boys agreed, and banded together to educate the little fellow. The bootblack became a learned man; and, better than that, a man of very beautiful character. He was George Whitefield, the great preacher.

* * * *

The testimony of that mighty man of God, D. L. Moody, is worthy of being repeated here.

I remember when I first went away from home. It was only twelve miles; but I've never been so far since as that seemed to me then. I had left my mother and sisters for the first time in my life, and if I ever needed a kind word or a word of cheer, it was then. I was walking down the street with my brother, who had gone there a year before; and as we were going along my brother said, pointing out an old gentleman, "There's a man that will give you a cent. He gives every new boy that comes to this town a cent. He gave me one, and I know he will you." I looked at him. I thought he was the finest-looking man I ever saw. When he came up to us he said to my brother, "Why, this is a new boy in the town, isn't it?" And he said, "Yes, sir. He's just come." He wanted him to be sure I hadn't got the cent. The old man took off my hat, and put his trembling hand on my head, and said, "Well, God bless you, my boy! I am told your father is dead; but you've got a Father in heaven." He gave me a brand-new cent. I don't know what has become of the cent; but I can feel the pressure of the old man's hand upon my head today. He gave me what I wanted so much — a kind and cheering word.

*   *   *   *

No one feels injustice more than does a child. Children shrink before slights. A sensitive girl or generous boy will glow with a sense of wrong or a feeling of ingratitude. Ill judged exactness is wicked, for the grief of a child is felt as heavily as a man's sorrow. Give the boy his kite and drum and give the girl her doll buggy and doll, and give both a kitten, a pup and a pigeon and watch the results.

A large portion of the miracles of Jesus were performed for the sake of youth. The widow's son still interests the Saviour. The ruler's daughter is still His delight. He still is welcoming the children and suffering them to come to Him.

Parents should never impatiently complain about the noise, pleasures or pastimes of their children. Such only need to be controlled. The future vacant chair and empty crib may break the heart. Children are a loan from God. They should be trained to trust and virtue, habitated to activity and industry and fired with ambition to be useful. A smileless, laughless child is a melancholy child and a melancholy child today is a possible suicide tomorrow. It is ten thousand pities to demand that children share our sorrows before they

are old enough to enter into our enjoyments. The frosts
of December may never nip the blossoms if there is
vigilance, care, diligence and kindness in April. How
much better to kiss away the tear and smile away the
hurt than to tell the child to shut up, or put a hand
over his mouth. How much better to lay a tender hand
on the head and breathe a simple prayer than to order
quietness or else . . .

* * * *

A drunkard who had run through his property, says
Dr. Schnebly, returned one night to his unfurnished
home. He entered its empty hall; anguish was gnawing
at his heart-strings, and l a n g u a g e is inadequate to
express his agony as he entered his wife's apartment,
and there beheld the victims of his appetite, his lovely
wife and darling child. Morose and sullen, he seated
himself without a word; he could not speak, he could
not look upon them. The mother said to the little angel
by her side, "Come, my child, it is time to go to bed";
and that little babe, as was her wont, knelt by her
mother's lap, and gazing wistfully into the face of her
suffering parent, like a piece of chiseled statuary, repeated her nightly orison; and when she had finished,
the child, (but four years of age,) said to her mother,
"Dear ma, may I not offer up one more prayer?" "Yes,
yes, my sweet pet, pray"; and she lifted up her tiny
hands, closed her eyes, and prayed, "O God! spare, oh,
spare my dear papa!" That prayer was wafted with
electric rapidity to the throne of God. It was heard on
high — 'twas heard on earth. The responsive "Amen"
burst from that father's lips, and his heart of stone

became a heart of flesh. Wife and child were both clasped to his bosom, and in penitence he said, *"My child, you have saved your father from the grave of a drunkard!"*

* * * *

A very profane and profligate sailor, who belonged to a vessel lying in the port of New York, went out one day from his ship into the streets, bent on folly and wickedness. He met a pious little girl, whose feelings he tried to wound by using vile and sinful language. The little girl looked at him earnestly in the face, warned him of his danger, and, with a solemn tone, told him to remember that he must meet her shortly at the bar of God. This unexpected reproof greatly affected him. To use his own language, "it was like a broadside, raking him fore and aft, and sweeping by the board every sail and spar prepared for a wicked cruise." Abashed and confounded, he returned to his ship. He could not banish from his mind the reproof of this little girl. Her look was present to his mind; her solemn declaration, "You must meet me at the bar of God," deeply affected his heart. The more he reflected upon it, the more uncomfortable he felt. In a few days his hard heart was subdued, and he submitted to the Savior. He became a consistent follower of the Lamb.

* * * *

Speaking on the question of child conversion the gifted and brilliant H. W. Beecher said, "Many persons are afraid of children's conversion. As though the conversion of a child that is free from the cares and

burdens which you carry like a hump on your back
was not more likely to be genuine than yours, if you
give it fair play! When little children think they are
converted people say, 'What, converted so small? Chris-
tians so young? Let us be careful. We will not take
them into the church yet. It will not do to bring them
along too fast. If they hold out we will receive them.'

"Suppose, a child being born, the doctor should say,
'My dear father and mother, it is uncertain whether
or not this child will live, and I advise you to put it
out on the front door-steps and leave it over night. If
it lives in the open air in January you may be sure
that it has a good constitution, and you will be war-
ranted in bringing it in and taking care of it.' Thus
you do a devilish work, and hope that God will do a
good one. Those periods when children feel drawings
toward higher things, and hear the call of God, are
just the periods when you should take care of them.
It is not hard to make a tree grow right if you begin
to train it when it is young, but to make a tree grow
right after you have allowed it to grow wrong till it
is old is not an easy matter."

* * * *

A certain business man has a curious little charm
for his watch chain. Business acquaintances often joke
him about it, for it is nothing but a queer little copper
two-cent piece, bright, it is true, through frequent
polishing, but plainly showing its value. Its v a l u e,
indeed! The man wouldn't sell it for a thousand dol-
lars. "I had lost every cent I had in the world, prac-

tically," he told some one with tears in his eyes, "and there at my desk, my head on my arms, I was thinking of a possible way to end it, when my little girl came up to me and asked a question: 'What does ruined mean, papa?' and then I knew I had been groaning loud enough to be heard and understood. 'You said "ruined," papa. What does ruin mean?' 'It means I haven't any money baby. Papa's a poor man.' The little feet pattered away, and then back again, and here on my watchchain is what she gave me. Not a great fortune — no, but the foundation of one. Whatever I've got since came from it, for it gave me courage."

*   *   *   *

"The mother of a family," writes A. Monod, "was married to an infidel, who made jest of religion in the presence of his own children; yet she succeeded in bringing them all up in the fear of the Lord. I asked her one day how she preserved them from the influence of a father whose sentiments were so opposed to her own. This was her answer: 'Because, to the authority of a father, I do not oppose the authority of a mother, but that of God. From their earliest years, my children have always seen the Bible upon my table. This holy book has constituted the whole of their religious instruction. I was silent, that I might allow it to speak. Did they propose a question, did they commit a fault, did they perform a good action, I opened the Bible, and the Bible answered, reproved or encouraged them. The constant reading of the Scriptures has wrought the prodigy which surprises you.'"

*   *   *   *

God pity the unloved child. Not even excepting the
delicate creature who gives it birth, the child is the
most delicate and sweetest thing in all the Universes
of God. To the fearless and faith-ful gaze of a child
the future looms up brilliant and beautiful as the dia-
mond studded walls of a fairy palace. Parents should
be ever gentle with children which a kindly Providence
has given to them. Children should be watched over
and cared for constantly and never for a moment wan-
tonly and heartlessly neglected. When necessary they
should be earnestly reproved but never in anger. An
angry mother or father is a murderer of the most
charming instincts in the breast of a babe. In the near
future the world will beat them up, bruise and batter
them a plenty. How forceful then are the Words of
God "Be not bitter against them." Children enlarge the
heart of those who love them. They give to the soul of
man higher aims because of their gentleness, simplicity
and worshipful trust and confidence.

*   *   *   *

A man once received from his own child, an infant
of three years old, one of the most severe reproofs he
ever met with. Family prayer had been, by some
means, neglected one morning, and the child was, as it
were, out of its element. At length, he came to his
father as he sat, and just as the family were going to
dinner, the little reprover, leaning on his father's knee,
said, with a sigh, "Pa, you were used to go to prayer
with us, but you did not today." "No, my dear," said
the parent, "I did not." "But, pa, you ought; why did

you not?" The father had not a word to reply, and the child's rebuke was as appropriate and natural, as if it had been administered by the most able minister in the land; and, it may be said, was as permanently useful.

*   *   *   *

Socrates once said, "Could I climb to the highest place in Athens, I would lift my voice and proclaim — Fellow-citizens, why do ye turn and scrape every stone to gather wealth, and take so little care of your children, to whom one day you must relinquish it all?"

*   *   *   *

Half the faults of children are the faults of their parents and grandparents, and the other half takes us back to the serpent in Eden. Most fathers expect more exemplary conduct from their children than they themselves exhibit. Mothers as a rule demand more from the child than was ever manifested by them.

*   *   *   *

A blacksmith, when he pulled his iron out of the fire, used to call out to his son, "Quick! quick! Now or never!" By this means he taught his son to strike the iron when it was hot, well knowing that if he once let it get cold, he should not be able to form it into a shoe. Now the disposition of a young person is somewhat like the hot iron; it can be easily bent into a proper form by education.

*   *   *   *

Some time ago three children — ten, seven, and four years old — arrived in St. Louis, having traveled all the way from Germany, without any escort or protection beyond a New Testament and their own innocence and helplessness. Their parents, who had emigrated from the Fatherland and settled in Missouri, left them in charge of an aunt, to whom they forwarded money sufficient to pay the expenses of the little ones to their new home across the Atlantic. As the children could not speak any other language than German, it is doubtful whether they would ever have reached their destination had not their aunt provided them with a passport, addressed not so much to an earthly authority as to Christian mankind generally. She gave the elder girl a New Testament, instructing her to show it to every person who might accost her, and especially to call their attention to the first leaf of the book. Upon that leaf were written the names of the three children, their birthplace and several ages, and this simple statement: — "Their father and mother in America are anxiously awaiting their arrival at Sedalia, Missouri." This was followed by the irresistible appeal — their guide, safeguard, and interpreter throughout a journey of more than four thousand miles — "Verily I say unto you, Inasmuch as ye have done it unto one of the least of these my brethren, ye have done it unto me." Many were the acts of kindness shown to the little travelers, many the hands held out to smooth their journey, until they reached their parents in perfect safety.

* * * *

The brilliant Dr. Finney of theological fame once remarked, "I am fond of children. I think them the

poetry of the world, the fresh flowers of our hearths
and homes; little conjurors, with their 'natural magic,'
evoking by their spells what delights and enriches all
ranks, and equalizes the different classes of society.
Often as they bring with them anxieties and cares, and
live to occasion sorrow and grief, we should get on very
badly without them. Only think, if there was never
anything anywhere to be seen, but great grown-up men
and women! How we should long for the sight of a
little child! Every infant comes into the world like a
delegated prophet, the harbinger and herald of good-
tidings, whose office it is 'to turn the hearts of the
fathers to the children,' and to draw 'the disobedient
to the wisdom of the just.' A child softens and purifies
the heart, warming and melting it by its gentle presence; it enriches the soul by new feelings, and awakens
within it what is favorable to virtue. It is a beam of
light, a fountain of love, a teacher whose lessons few
can resist. Infants recall us from much that engenders
and encourages selfishness, that freezes the affections,
roughens the manners, indurates the heart: they
brighten the home, deepen love, invigorate exertion, in-
fuse courage, and vivify and sustain the charities of
life. It would be a terrible world, I do think, if it was
not embellished by little children!"

*   *   *   *

A mother whose children were remarkable examples
of early piety, was asked the secret of her success. She
answered, "While my children were infants on my lap,
as I washed them, I raised my heart to God, that he

would wash them in that blood which cleanseth from all sin; as I clothed them in the morning, I asked my Heavenly Father to clothe them with the robe of Christ's righteousness; as I provided them food, I prayed that God would feed their souls with the bread of heaven, and give them to drink of the water of life. When I have prepared them for the house of God, I have pleaded that their bodies might be fit temples for the Holy Ghost to dwell in. When they left me for the week-day school, I followed their infant footsteps with a prayer, that their path through life might be like that of the just, which shineth more and more unto the perfect day. And as I committed them to the rest of the night, the silent breathing of my soul has been, that their Heavenly Father would take them to his embrace, and fold them in his paternal arms."

* * * *

We are prone to forget the bridges that have been built for us by the generations that have gone on before us. We are prone to forget the "Appleseed Johnnies," the "Pioneers," the "Missionaries," the "Scouts" who have paced the way; those who have "cleared a free way for the feet of God." But a poem like the "Bridge Builder," by Will Allen Dromgoole, makes us remember to whom we owe our tribute of praise and affection; to our fathers and our mothers; to those others who have gone before us and made the hard ways easier for us.

An old man, going a lone highway,
Came at the evening cold and gray
To a chasm vast and deep and wide,

Through which was flowing a sullen tide.
The old man crossed in the twilight dim,
The sullen stream had no fears for him;
But he turned when safe on the other side
And built a bridge to span the tide.
"Old man," said a fellow pilgrim near,
"You are wasting your strength with building here;
Your journey will end with the ending day;
You never again will pass this way;
You have passed the chasm deep and wide;
Why build you the bridge at eventide?"

The builder lifted his old gray head—
"There followeth after me a youth,
Whose feet must pass this way forsooth;
This chasm that has been naught to me,
To that fairhaired youth may a pitfall be;
He, too, must cross in the twilight dim;
Good friend, I am building the bridge for him."

* * * *

Pitt, who was Prime Minister of England when twenty-four, was once taunted by an old man with his extreme youth. "The atrocious crime of being a young man," he said, "I shall not attempt to palliate or deny, but content myself with wishing that I may be one of those whose follies may cease with their youth, and not of that number who are ignorant in spite of experience."

* * * *

"Beyond all doubt," says Nehemiah Boyn, "blood tells. Our ancestors sow for us the harvests that bless or the harvests that blight. Visitors to the upper dome of the mosque in St. Petersburg tell us that the myriad sounds of the multitudes upon the pavement hundreds of feet beneath are so brought together as to become like unto music. Thus, if we put our ear to the child's nature, we shall hear the reverberations of the vast and distant multitudes; the groans and sobs of sin and suffering; the sounds of joy and laughter, sounding down the long aisles of the past. Coleridge the elder was an opium-eater, and Hartley, his son, inherited the same intense craving, as did another after him. The reason for this, according to Fiske, is by means of the lengthened period of dependence to develop and strengthen the 'other regarding feelings' in the primitive parents. Here at least is the beginning of the idea of the human family, when parents put their rude strength and prowess at the disposal, though in very meager fashion at first, of the helpless and dependent offspring.

* * * *

Be kind to your baby. Be considerate toward your child. The very helpfulness of the child should appeal to kindly hearts for special consideration and kindness. Be kind to your child. Your boy is only a baby once and only for a very brief and swiftly passing day. The world will treat him roughly tomorrow. Be kind to him today. Your little girl will soon be the recipient of more heartbreaks than will be her due. The world will soon trample upon her innocence and virtue. Be kind to her now. She will be kicked and cuffed tomorrow. Be kind to her today. Be kind to your child.

> When the lessons all are ended,
> And the school for the day is dismissed,
> And the little ones gather around me

To bid me good-night and be kissed;
Oh! the little white arms that encircle
My neck in a tender embrace!
Oh! the smiles that are halos of Heaven
Shedding sunshine of joy on my face!

And when they are gone I sit dreaming
Of my childhood, too lovely to last;
Of love that my heart well remembers
When it wakes to the pulse of the past,
Ere the world and its wickedness made me
A portion of sorrow and sin—
When the glory of God was about me,
And the glory of gladness within.

Oh! my heart grows as weak as a woman's,
And the fountain of feeling will flow
When I think of the path, steep and stony,
Where the feet of the dear ones must go;
Of the mountains of sin hanging o'er them,
Of the tempest of fate blowing wild;
Oh! there's nothing on earth half so holy
As the innocent heart of a child.

They are idols of hearts and of households;
They are angels of God, in disguise;
His sunlight still sleeps in their tresses,
His glory still gleams in their eyes.
Oh! those truants from home and from Heaven,
They make me more manly and mild;
And I know now how Jesus can liken
The kingdom of God to a child.

I ask not a life for the dear ones,
All radiant, as others have done;
But that life may have just enough shadow
To temper the glare of the sun.

I would pray God to guard them from evil—
But my prayer would bound back to myself—
Ah! a seraph can pray for a sinner,

But a sinner must pray for himself.
The twig is so easily bended,
    I have banished the rule and the rod;
I have taught them the goodness of knowledge
    They have taught me the goodness of God.
My heart is a dungeon of darkness
    When I shut them from breaking a rule;
My frown is sufficient correction—
    My love is the law of the school.

I shall leave the old house in the autumn
    To traverse its threshold no more.
Ah! how I shall sigh for the dear ones
    That meet me each morn at the door!
I shall miss the "good-nights" and the kisses,
    And the gush of their innocent glee,
The group on the green, and the flowers
    That are brought every morning to me.

I shall miss them at morn and at even,
    Their song in the school and the street;
I shall miss the low hum of their voices,
    And the tramp of their delicate feet.
When the lessons and tasks are all ended,
    And death says, "The school is dismissed,"
May the little ones gather around me
    To bid me good-night and be kissed.

                    —Charles Dickinson

CHAPTER V

HELPS TO HUSBANDS

A GOOD, sweet and loving wife is a gift from God and bestowed upon a man to help turn the wilderness of his life to an earthly paradise preparatory to the Paradise above. One of the most exquisite and wonderful things in the life of a real man is the unclouded welcome home from a loving wife. The husband may not know it but it certainly pays good dividends to deal kindly with the wife of one's youth. Do not blame your wife if she is miserable or a clown or unhappy unless you are quite sure she is not mated to a clown, to misery or unhappiness. If your wife acts like a little girl it may be that she just married an overgrown boy. Marriage is beyond doubt the best state for a man in general. A man is a worse man in proportion as he is unfit for the marriage altar, the marriage vow and the marriage state. A husband, a real he-man, is to be a loving LORD, an unselfish and serving GOVERNOR, a kindly, gracious and considerate KING to the sweet and noble spirit who commits herself into his hands. A little more doting over a dutiful wife and a little less doubting of her abilities, qualities and motives would help to sweeten both hearth and home.

The Husband at the head of the home can mar or make the happiness of the household. Kindness pays high dividends and offers rich and lasting rewards.

*   *   *   *

Do you know you have asked for the costliest thing
    Ever made by the Hand above—
A woman's heart and a woman's life
    And a woman's wonderful love?

Do you know you have asked for this priceless thing
    As a child might ask for a toy?
Demanding what others have died to win
    With the reckless dash of a boy!

You have written my lesson of duty out;
    Man-like, you have questioned me.
Now stand at the bar of my woman's soul
    Until I shall question thee.

You require your mutton shall always be hot;
    Your socks and your shirts shall be whole.
I require your heart shall be true as God's stars;
    And pure as Heaven your soul.

I am fair and young, but the rose will fade
    From my soft, young cheek one day.
Will you love me then, 'mid the falling leaves,
    As you did 'mid the bloom of May?

Is your heart an ocean so strong and deep
    I may launch my all on its tide?
A loving woman finds Heaven or hell
    On the day she is made a bride.

I require all things that are grand and true;
    All things that a man should be.
If you give this all I would stake my life
    To be all you demand of me.

If you can not do this, a laundress and cook
    You can hire with little to pay;
But a woman's heart and a woman's life
    Are not to be won that way.

*   *   *   *

Does it not seem strange that to some husbands the OTHER woman is the only woman for them. The year that they are married something seems to happen to the wife, some tremendous revolution seizes her system, all her good and previously perennial qualities suddenly vanish, like eggs out of the hat of the conjuror. To such a husband the eggs are gone forever. He once thought he could never be happy without his brunette, but now it is a blonde. Once it was his only slender and youthful friend but now its the plump, round and giddy painted fool.

The husband may not realize it, but save the love we pay to high heaven, there is none purer, none holier and none more sublime than that which a virtuous woman feels for the man to whom she has pledged her allegiance. The worth while girl, when she finds the worth while boy, worships at his shrine.

We men should bear it everlastingly in mind that when a woman loves and finds her love reciprocated she is a servant and a worshipper of the man to whom she is wed. From such a gentle and affectionate soul there can spring that which is good always. Time, to such an one, secretly strengthens the solemn tie that binds. What a delight to kiss away the sparkling tears from such adoring and tender eyes. What a light shining in the home in the darkest and dreariest nights. What an angel presiding over the life and pilgrimage of a man, dividing his cares and doubling his pleasures. What an unspeakable calamity to betray such confidence and kill such love. Marriage is the purest tie of perpetual friendship and the man must expect to be doubly wretched who pays to beauty, riches or passing politeness the regard and attention which only virtue, purity and piety should receive.

*   *   *   *

Emerson says: "Do not hang a dismal picture on your wall, and do not deal with sable and glooms in your conversation." Beecher follows: "Away with these fellows who go howling through life, and all the while passing for Birds of Paradise. He that cannot laugh and be gay, should look to himself. He should fast and pray until his face breaks forth into light." Talmage then takes up the strain: "Some people have an idea that they comfort the afflicted when they groan over them. Don't drive a hearse through a man's soul. When you bind up a broken bone of the soul, and you want splints, do not make them out of cast iron." Hume, the historian, said that the habit of looking at the bright side of things was better than an income of a thousand a year. It was said of Cromwell that hope shone like a fiery pillar in him when it had gone out in all others.

*   *   *   *

The command of the apostle, "Be not unequally yoked together with unbelievers," obtains its validity from the fact that where there is no true union of soul there can be no lasting union at all — none of that deep mutual sympathy with and understanding of each other which are necessary to life's companionship.

This truth is suggested in a modern picture which represents two lovers seated in a room. They are engaged in conversation, and into it the youth is pouring his whole soul. He is speaking to her of his ideals, his ambitions and longings, and the pale, ascetic face indicates that these are not material, but lofty and ideal. The girl is pretty and well-meaning, but her face has no depth. She loves him and strives to sympathize and understand, but it is all beyond her depth and a trifle wearisome, and she cannot keep her mind from wandering to take notice of the ring on her finger, which tells her that she is actually engaged! It is not difficult to see that these two are "unequally yoked"; in after days they will drift apart, perhaps both becoming embittered. It is only to be hoped that they will find it out before it be too late.

* * * *

"What you want, O man!" declared Dr. Talmage, "in a wife, is not a butterfly of the sunshine, not a giggling nonentity, not a painted doll, not a gossiping gadabout, not a mixture of artificialities which leave you in doubt as to where the humbug ends and the woman begins, but an earnest soul, one that cannot only laugh when you laugh, but weep when you weep. There will be wide, deep graves in your path of life, and you will both want steadying when you come to the verge of them, I tell you. When your fortune fails you will want some one to talk of treasures in heaven, and not charge upon you with a bitter, 'I told you so.' As far as I can analyze it, *sincerity and earnestness* are the foundation of all worthy wifehood. Get that, and you get all. Fail to get that, and you get nothing but what you will wish you never had got."

* * * *

A good and thoughtful husband will never reprove his wife in the presence of a third party. He will constantly bear in mind that a dutiful wife is heaven's last and noblest gift to man, that she is at once his angel and minister, his gem of many graces, his casket of priceless jewels, and the guardian of his home and honor. The voice of a happy wife is music to the ears of a weary, burdened, horny-handed husband. The smiles of a loving bride make his brightest and best days. The breath of such a helpmeet is a balsam to his big heart. The industry and economy of such a confident is his surest wealth and safest bank, and her prayers should bring heaven's blessing upon his head and take the lead out of his heels. We should not however deceive ourselves into a false belief that marriage is the summum-bonum of life. Full contentment, happiness, peace and joy is found only in Christ, a holy heart and a holy life.

* * * *

CHAPTER VI

WORDS OF WISDOM TO WIVES

AN obedient, happy and holy wife commands her husband. Sarah called Abraham her lord and she was the supreme dictator. Man was intended by the Creator to be a circled oak with woman the clinging and lasting ivy. A husband is not a meal ticket. A wife is not to be a gold digger. She is not to measure his love by his gifts or the fine home and table which he may provide. He is not intended to be a plaster for all her ills, or a banking account from which she may pay all her debts and desires. One reason why so few marriages are successful is because young women spend so much of their courtship time in making a net instead of a cage. Flippancy and fun are poor foundations for a full life. Do not act as though you would have enjoyed being married to a POEM or given away by a NOVEL or it is possible that you may build a man of snow and then of course when he melts you must weep.

A good and worth while wife is like the green ivy which beautifies the building to which it clings. The ivy seems to twine its tendrils more lovingly as time ages and ruins the edifice. The wife should be the last one in the world to wage war in the home or seek for rule, supremacy or sway. Her affectionate heart was made for peace, love, obedience, service and prayer. Of all creatures, she should seek peace and

pursue it. To fulfill her destiny she must follow peace
and holiness without which there is no happiness here
and no heaven hereafter.

Do not rail and brawl and otherwise be clamorous,
unless you wish to destroy the only treasure you
possess, next to God and holiness — a woman's heart.

* * * *

"Marriage," wrote Dr. Jeremy Taylor, "has in it less
of beauty, but more of safety, than the single life; it
hath not more ease, but less danger; it is more merry
and more sad; it is fuller of sorrows and fuller of joys;
it lies under more burdens, but is supported by all the
strengths of love and charity; and those burdens are
delightful. Marriage is the mother of the world, and
preserves kingdoms, and fills cities and churches, and
heaven itself. Celibacy, like the fly in the heart of an
apple, dwells in perpetual sweetness, but sits alone, and
is confined and dies in singularity; but marriage, like
the useful bee, builds a house, and gathers sweetness
from every flower, and labors and unities into societies
and republics, and sends out colonies, and feeds the
world with delicacies, and obeys the king, and keeps
order, and exercises many virtues, and promotes the
interest of mankind, and is that state of good to which
God hath designed the present constitution of the
world."

* * * *

What the bow is to the violin, so is a loving and
winsome wife to a man. Obeying him she bends him,
drawing him as by unseen cords. He follows and each

is incomplete without the other. One mistake, which many make is in regarding marriage as a scheme of happiness, a something which gives ease, pleasure, or freedom from labor and care. Marriage is a bond of usefulness and service. It is the most ancient form of ministry to which all are ordained.

It is at once the greatness and glory of a real wife when she sets herself the task of making the boy into a man, the dwarf into a giant, the slouch into a sober, well groomed citizen, the earthly redeemer of the race.

The real wife is the bigger better-part to the blessed man but if frowning, peevish, sour or sullen she becomes a grief in the morning and a pain in the night. The good wife is none of our dainty painted women, who desire only to appear in a different dress at every meal. The dutiful and thoughtful wife will set her sail according to the keel of her income and not according to the whims and wishes of the neighbors. To be good humored, peaceful, thrifty, affable, discreet, neat, tidy, forgiving, patient and joyful is not to be an angel as some suppose, but to be the fulfillment of the dreams of youth. Forget the frailties and faults and dwell on the delights and fruitful duties of both the home and Church, and happiness will increase as the years come and go. Not a small part of the uneasiness and storms on the matrimonial sea arise from mere trifles. In such cases the one who is surely convinced to be in the right should always surrender. To be big, one must give little victories to the other.

*   *   *   *

"I charge also the wife," says Talmage, "to keep

herself as attractive after marrige as she was before
marriage. The reason that so often a man ceases to
love his wife is because the wife ceases to be lovable.
In many cases what elaboration of toilet before marriage, and what recklessness of appearance after! *The
most disgusting thing on earth* is a slatternly woman
— I mean a woman who never combs her hair until
she goes out, or looks like a fright until somebody calls.
That a man married to one of these creatures stays at
home as little as possible is no wonder. It is a wonder
that such a man does not go on a whaling voyage of
three years, and in a leaky ship. Costly wardrobe is
not required; but, O woman! if you are not willing,
by all that ingenuity of refinement can effect, to make
yourself attractive to your husband, you ought not
to complain if he seeks in other society those pleasant
surroundings which you deny him."

* * * *

"The need of divine direction I argue from the fact
that so many men, and some of them strong and wise,
have wrecked their lives at this juncture," says Talmage. "Witness Samson and this woman of Timnath!
Witness *Socrates*, pecked of the historical Xantippe!
Witness *Job*, whose wife had nothing to prescribe for
his carbuncles but allopathic doses of profanity! Witness *Ananias*, a liar, who might perhaps have been
cured by a truthful spouse, yet marrying as great a
liar as himself — Sapphira! Witness *John Wesley*,
one of the best men that ever lived, united to one of
the most outrageous and scandalous of women, who

sat in City Road Chapel making mouths at him while he preached! Witness the once connubial wretchedness of *John Ruskin,* the great art essayist, and *Frederick W. Robertson,* the great preacher.

When a man falls into misfortune his spirits may be soothed, his mind changed, his outlook brightened, his uplook enlarged and his whole situation retrieved by a winsome wife. She may keep alive man's self respect when all around is dismal, dreary and dark. In his own home and with his wife he will find a world of love and peace over which he may feel once again that he is a king. A real honest to goodness woman will compel a real he-man to exertions of which he hardly thinks himself capable. Many a coward at heart has been made a confirmed hero not for himself but for his wife and children. Thinking of wife and home has held him steady through many a storm. A wife does far more to support the man than the man does to support his wife.

The wise and happy wife will not only keep an immaculately clean body and home, but will be modest and chaste and wearing the ornament of a meek and quiet spirit; she will become to her husband of great price. These are a few of the things which make a wife pleasant while she lives and desired after she dies. — Nay, such an one never dies.

* * * *

TWENTY SECRETS OF SUCCESS

1. The very nearest approach to d o m e s t i c happiness on earth is in the cultivation on both sides of absolute unselfishness.

2. Never both be angry at once.

3. Never talk at one another, either alone or in company.

4. Never speak loudly to one another unless the house is on fire.

5. Let each one strive to yield oftenest to the wishes of the other.

6. Let self-denial be the daily aim and practice of each.

7. Never find fault unless it is perfectly certain that a fault has been committed, and always speak lovingly.

8. Never taunt with a past mistake.

9. Neglect the whole world besides rather than one another.

10. Never allow a request to be repeated.

11. Never make a remark at the expense of each other—it is a meanness.

12. Never part for a day without loving words to think of during absence.

13. Never meet without a loving welcome.

14. Never let the sun go down upon any anger or grievance.

15. Never let any fault you have committed go by until you have frankly confessed it and asked forgiveness.

16. Never forget the happy hours of early love.

17. Never sigh over what might have been, but make the best of what is.

18. Never forget that marriage is ordained of God, and that His blessing alone can make it what it should ever be.

19. Never be contented till you know you are both walking in the narrow way.

20. Never let your hopes stop short of the eternal home.

* * * *

Dear Chloe, while the busy crowd,
The vain, the wealthy, and the proud,
    In folly's maze advance;
Though singularity and pride
Be called our choice, we'll step aside,
    Nor join the giddy dance.

From the gay world we'll oft retire
To our own family and fire,
    Where love our hours employ;
No noisy neighbor enters here,
No intermeddling stranger near,
    To spoil our heartfelt joys.

If solid happiness we prize,
Within our breast this jewel lies,
    And they are fools who roam;
The world hath nothing to bestow—
From our own selves our bliss must flow,
    And that dear hut, our home.

*   *   *   *

An ear that waits to catch
A hand upon the latch;
A step that hastens its sweet rest to win.
A world of cares without;
A world of strife shut out;
A world of love shut in.
Two birds within one nest;
Two hearts within one breast;
Two souls within one fair,
Firm league of love and prayer,
Together bound for aye, together blest.

*   *   *   *

A CLOSING WORD

Wife, be patient with your husband. You will never know the heartaches endured by him in order to keep bread and milk on your table.

Husband, be affectionate and fore-bearing toward your wife. You will never know how much and how deeply she has suffered. You will never know how many steps it takes to be a real wife and a true mother.

Parents, be kind to your babies. The world will soon buffet and break their little hearts. At the cemetery you will regret every unnecessary slap or slight given them.

Children, be thoughtful of your parents and obey them in the Lord. They are your very best friends. Be kindly affectioned one toward another and so home a stepping stone toward HEAVEN.

*   *   *   *

Chapter VII

THOUGHTS FROM OTHER THINKERS

OH! Surely marriage is a great and sacred respon-
sibility. It is a bark in which two souls venture
out on life's stormy sea, with no aid but their own
to help them; the well-doing of their frail vessel must
in future solely rest upon themselves; no one can take
part either to mar or make their bliss or misery.

J. Hamilton.

* * * *

In wedlock to love is a far greater blessing than to
be beloved, since it preserves and keeps people from
falling into many errors — nay, all those that corrupt
and ruin matrimony.

Plutarch.

* * * *

If you are for pleasure, marry; if you prize rosy
health, marry. A good wife is heaven's last best gift
to a man; his angel of mercy; minister of graces innumerable; his gem of many virtues; his casket of
jewels; her voice, his sweetest music; her smiles, his
brightest day; her kiss, the guardian of innocence; her
arms, the pale of his safety, the balm of his health, the
balsam of his life; her industry, his surest wealth; her
economy, his s a f e s t steward; her lips, his faithful
counsellors; her bosom, the softest pillow of his cares;

and her prayers, the ablest advocates of Heaven's blessing on his head.

Bishop Taylor.

*   *   *   *

As the Lord commanded that an ox and an ass should not be yoked together, because the match is unequal; even so it is an unlawful thing for the faithful to marry with infidels, or to have anything else to do with them.

Cawdray.

*   *   *   *

Marriage is a desperate thing. The frogs in Æsop were extremely wise: they had a great mind to some water; but they would not leap into the well, because they could not get out again.

Selden.

*   *   *   *

Sweet are the joys of Home,
    And pure as sweet; for they,
Like dews of morn and evening, come
    To wake and close the day.

The world hath its delights,
    And its delusions, too;
But Home to calmer bliss invites,
    More tranquil and more true.

The mountain flood is strong,
    But fearful in its pride;
While gently rolls the stream along
    The peaceful valley's side.

Life's charities, like light,
    Spread smilingly afar;
But stars approached, become more bright,
    And Home is life's own star.

> The pilgrim's step in vain
>   Seeks Eden's sacred ground!
> But in Home's holy joys, again
>   An Eden may be found.
>
> A glance of heaven to see,
>   To none on earth is given;
> And yet a happy family
>   Is but an earlier heaven.
>
> *John Bowring*

* * * *

Encourage that which you see good and commendable in your children. *Virtus laudata crescit.* Commending that which is good in your children, makes them more in love with virtuous actions; and is like the watering of plants, which makes them grow more.

Watson, 1696.

* * * *

Mothers who force their daughters into interested marriage are worse than the Ammonites, who sacrificed their children to Moloch, — the latter undergoing a speedy death; the former suffering years of torture, but too frequently leading to the same result.

Lord Rochester.

* * * *

Take the daughter of a good mother.—*Fuller.* Never marry but for love; but see that thou lovest what is lovely. — *William Penn.* If you wish to marry suitably, marry your equal. — *Ovid.* Hasty marriage seldom proveth well. — *Shakespeare.*

You have tied a knot with your tongue you cannot undo with your teeth. A man's best fortune or his worst is his wife.—*English*. He that goes far to marry goes to be deceived or to deceive. The day you marry you kill or cure yourself.—*Spanish*. Before you marry, have where to tarry. — *Italian*. It is easier to build two hearths than always to have a fire on one. — *German*.

* * * *

The worst predicament possible is to be unhappily yoked together. You see it is impossible to break the yoke. The more you pull apart, the more galling the yoke. The minister might bring you up again, and in your presence read the marriage ceremony backward, might put you on the opposite sides of the altar from where you were when you were united, might take the ring off of the finger, might rend the wedding veil asunder, might tear out the marriage leaf from the family Bible record, but all that would fail to unmarry you. It is better not to make the mistake than to attempt its correction. But men and women do not reveal all their characteristics till after marriage, and how are you to avoid committing the fatal blunder? There is only one Being in the universe who can tell you whom to choose, and that is the Lord of Paradise. He made Eve for Adam, and Adam for Eve, and both for each other.

* * * *

Few special days in the average Sunday school are looked forward to with such eager expectancy on the part of the scholars as Children's Day. Even fathers and mothers, big brothers and sisters, who perhaps seldom enter church doors, go then if at no other time. With many schools it is practically the end of a year's work and an anniversary corresponding to Commencement Day in our public schools. But in every school it may be a day of unusual opportunity for presenting the joy of the Christ-life and the friendship of the All-Loving One to many who perhaps are not reached at other times during the year. — *New Century Teacher's Monthly.*

* * * *

But these dear boys and girls — there is something to be made out of them. If now they yield themselves to Christ they may have a long, happy and holy day before them in which they may serve God with all their hearts. Who knows what glory God may have of them? Heathen lands may call them blessed. Whole nations may be enlightened by them. O brethren and sisters, let us estimate children at their true valuation, and we shall not keep them back, but we shall be eager to lead them to Jesus at once.

Spurgeon.

* * * *

Do not others expect from children more perfect conduct than they themselves exhibit? If a gracious child should lose his temper or act wrongly in some trifling thing through forgetfulness, straightway he is condemned as a little hypocrite by those who are a long way from being perfect themselves. Jesus says, "Take heed that ye despise not one of these little ones."

Spurgeon.

* * * *

"Suffer that little children come to Me,
Forbid them not." Emboldened by His words,
The mothers onward press; but, finding vain
The attempt to reach the Lord, they trust their babes
To strangers' hands; the innocents, alarmed
Amid the throng of faces all unknown,
Shrink, trembling, till their wandering eyes discern
The countenance of Jesus, beaming love
And pity; eager then they stretch their arms,
And, cowering, lay their heads upon His breast.

—James Grahame

* * * *

Ought there to be room in the bonds of church-fellowship for the great mass of average boys and girls who, by judicious training and careful Christian nurture, may be induced very early to give their hearts to God? Aye, we believe with all our heart there ought to be such a place. We believe that before many years there will be such a place in every true church, and it will be just as much expected that many young children will form part of the membership of every church as that there will be gray-haired men and women there.

Rev. F. E. Clark, D. D.

* * * *

When children ask you questions about gray hairs, and wrinkles in the face, and sighs that have no words, and smiles too bright to be carved upon the radiant face by the hands of hypocrisy — when they ask you about kneeling at the altar, speaking into the vacant air, and uttering words to an unseen and in an invisible Presence — when they interrogate you about your great psalms, and hymns, and anthem-bursts of thank-

fulness, what is your reply to these? Do not be ashamed
of the history. Keep steadily along the line of fact.
Say what happened to you, and magnify God in the
hearing of the inquirer.

Rev. Joseph Parker.

* * * *

If I knew you and you knew me —
If both of us could clearly see,
And with an inner sight divine
The meaning of your heart and mine,
I'm sure that we would differ less
And clasp our hands in friendliness;
Our thoughts would pleasantly agree
If I knew you and you knew me,

If I knew you and you knew me,
As each one knows his own self, we
Could look each other in the face
And see therein a truer grace.
Life has so many hidden woes,
So many thorns, for every rose;
The "why" of things our hearts would see,
If I knew you and you knew me.

— Nixon Waterman

* * * *

THE PRICE HE PAID

I said I would have my fling,
And do what a young man may:
And I didn't believe a thing
That the parsons have to say.
I didn't believe in a God
That gives us blood like fire,
Then flings us into hell because
We answer the call of desire.

And I said "Religion is rot,
And the laws of the world are nil:

For the bad man is he who is caught
And cannot foot his bill.
And there is no place called hell:
And heaven is only a truth,
And when a man has his way with a maid,
In the fresh keen hour of youth.

"And money can buy us grace,
If it rings on the plate of the church:
And money can neatly erase,
Each sign of a sinful smirch."
For I saw men everywhere,
Hotfooting the road of vice;
And women and preachers smiled on them
As long as they paid the price.

So I had my joy of life:
I went the pace of the town;
And then I took me a wife,
And started to settle down.
I had gold enough and to spare
For all of the simple joys
That belong with a house and a home
And a brood of girls and boys.

I married a girl with health
And virtue and spotless fame,
I gave in exchange my wealth
And a proud old family name.
And I gave her the love of a heart
Grown sated and sick of sin!
My deal with the devil was all cleaned up,
And the last bill handed in.

And she was going to bring me a child,
And when in labor she cried,
With love an fear I was wild—
But now I wish she had died.
For the son she bore me was blind

And crippled and weak and sore!
And his mother was left a wreck.
It was so *she* settled my score.

I said I must have my fling,
And they knew the path I would go;
Yet no one told me a thing
Of what I needed to know.
Folks talk too much of a soul
From heavenly joys debarred —
And not enough of the babes unborn,
By the sins of their fathers scarred.

— *Ella Wheeler Wilcox*

* * * *

We speak of educating our children. Do we know that our children also educate us?

Mrs. Sigourney.

* * * *

Let us be men with men, and always children before God; for in His eyes we are but children. Old age itself, in presence of eternity is but the first moment of a morning.

Joseph Joubert.

* * * *

I never hear parents exclaim impatiently, "Children, you must not make so much noise," that I do not think how soon the time may come when, beside the vacant seat, those parents would give *all the world,* could they hear once more the ringing laughter which once so disturbed them.

A. E. Kittredge.

* * * *

Let your children be as so many flowers, borrowed from God. If the flowers die or wither, thank God for a Summer loan of them.

Rutherford.

*   *   *   *

A *happy home* is the single spot of rest which a man has upon this earth for the cultivation of his noblest sensibilities.

F. W. Robertson.

*   *   *   *

There is no happiness in life, there is no misery like that growing out of the dispositions which consecrate or desecrate a home.

E. H. Chapin.

*   *   *   *

When home is ruled according to God's word, angels might be asked to stay a night with us, and they would not find themselves out of their element.

C. H. Spurgeon.

*   *   *   *

In the homes of America are born the children of America; and from them go out into American life, American men and women. They go out with the stamp of these homes upon them; and only as these homes are what they should be, will *they* be what they should be.

J. G. Holland.

*   *   *   *

The strength of a nation, especially of a republican nation, is in the intelligent and well-ordered homes of the people.

Mrs. Sigourney.

*   *   *   *

A Christian home! What a power it is to the child when he is far away in the cold, tempting world, and voices of sin are filling his ears, and his feet stand on slippery places.

A. E. Kittredge.

*   *   *   *

The spirit and tone of your home will have great influence on your children. If it is what it ought to be, it will fasten conviction on their minds, however wicked they may become.

Richard Cecil.

*   *   *   *

The pleasant converse of the fireside, the simple songs of home, the words of encouragement as I bend over my school-tasks, the kiss as I lie down to rest, the patient bearing with the freaks of my restless nature, the gentle counsels mingled with reproofs and approvals, the sympathy that meets and assuages every sorrow, and sweetens every little success — all these return to me amid the responsibilities which press upon me now, and I feel as if I had once lived in heaven, and, straying, had lost my way.

J. G. Holland.

*   *   *   *

I never heard my father's or mother's voice once raised in any question with each other; nor saw any

angry or even slightly hurt or offended glance in the
eyes of either. I never heard a servant scolded, nor
even suddenly, passionately, or in any severe manner,
blamed; and I never saw a moment's trouble or dis-
order in any household matter.

John Ruskin.

* * * *

It is to Jesus Christ we owe the truth, the tenderness, the purity, the warm affection, the holy aspira-
tion, which go together in that endearing word—home;
for it is He who has made obedience so beautiful, and
affection so holy; it is He who has brought the Father's
home so near, and has taught us that love is of God.

James Hamilton.

* * * *

The sweetest type of heaven is home — nay, heaven
is the home for whose acquisition we are to strive the
most strongly. Home, in one form and another, is the
great object of life. It stands at the end of every day's
labor, and beckons us to its bosom; and life would be
cheerless and meaningless, did we not discern across
the river that divides us from the life beyond, glimpses
of the pleasant mansions prepared for us.

J. G. Holland.

* * * *